Elements of Human and Social Geography

Some Anthropological Perspectives

Elements of Human and Social Geography

Some Anthropological Perspectives

ERIC SUNDERLAND
Professor of Anthropology, University of Durham

PERGAMON PRESS

OXFORD · NEW YORK · TORONTO
SYDNEY · BRAUNSCHWEIG

Pergamon Press Ltd., Headington Hill Hall, Oxford
Pergamon Press Inc., Maxwell House, Fairview Park, Elmsford,
New York 10523
Pergamon of Canada Ltd., 207 Queen's Quay West, Toronto 1
Pergamon Press (Aust.) Pty. Ltd., 19a Boundary Street,
Rushcutters Bay, N.S.W. 2011, Australia
Vieweg & Sohn GmbH, Burgplatz 1, Braunschweig

First edition 1973

Library of Congress Cataloging in Publication Data
Sunderland, Eric.
Elements of human and social geography.
(The Commonwealth and international library,
Pergamon Oxford geographies)
Includes bibliographical references.
1. Anthropology   1. Title.
GN31.S83 1973   301.2   73–10060
ISBN 0–08–017689–5
ISBN 0–08–017690–9 (flexicover)

*Printed in Great Britain by
Western Printing Services Ltd., Bristol*

Contents

v

List of Tables

List of Figures

Introduction

FOR some years the author has taught a large class of first-year under-graduates in the University of Durham, the course of lectures being termed "An Introduction to Anthropology". Students proposing later to specialize in Anthropology or in a number of other disciplines, including Geography, attend the course, many aspects of which are dealt with in this book.

In Anthropology, Geography, Psychology and other related social sciences it is interesting and illuminating to comprehend something of man's animal origin, his primate background, since that animal origin can not be denied and still exercises some influence on the patterns of social behaviour in human groups today. The importance of this background has often been underestimated but Tiger and Fox (1972) have clearly demonstrated its significance in their recent book.

However, man is, by definition, a social animal and hence much of this book must concern itself with aspects of socialization. The earliest undoubted hominids, the Australopithecinae, were able to survive in a terrestrial habitat because of their capacity to co-operate systematically with one another, to live in groups and thus to compete successfully with carnivores and to overcome other environmental hazards. Once these intelligent, tool-using, social animals were "established" in East Africa in lower Pleistocene times their more advanced descendants were soon to spread rapidly into other parts of the Old World. By the Middle Pleistocene, occupying areas as far north as the United Kingdom and northern China, they had broken out of the tropical habitats where all the earlier hominids and indeed all the earlier primates had lived.

Throughout most of man's existence hunting and gathering constituted the economic basis for existence. This was everywhere the case until some 10,000 years ago and small groups survive to this day who live in this manner, usually in remote and inhospitable regions. However, approximately 10,000 years ago dramatic changes occurred in this regard—the so-called Neolithic Revolution. Communities appeared in the Middle East which, though engaging in some hunting and gathering, secured most of their food supply by cultivating crops and by keeping domesticated animals. These revolutionary practices were to have profound consequences for social life generally. Food surpluses which could be stored might fairly readily be produced and this efficient economic practice made possible the appearance of non-food producing specialists skilled at the manufacture of tools, administration, fighting or ritual expertise, all ultimately maintained by the transfer of wealth from the primary producers. This complex pattern of social interaction as a way of life was usually found in villages and towns and it soon spread to many other parts of the world from its original homeland in the Middle East. Such socio-cultural diffusion is well illustrated by the known sequences dated at European sites.

Despite the rapid spread of the whole Neolithic way of life to many areas, communities survive to this day who have adopted but a part of the complex, possibly because of environmental difficulties. Tribal groups of pastoral nomads or of cultivators occur widely but a major fraction of the world's populace consists of peasant-cultivators—individuals with a long-enduring, stable relationship with the small area of land from which they and their forefathers secured a living. In this book the peasant way of life has been briefly described, principally with reference to Middle Eastern communities, though many of the basic field studies have been undertaken in the New World.

From these peasant societies more complex politico-economic units were to emerge, including the nation-state in due course of time. The present book stops short of a consideration of these latter-day complexities. Nevertheless, it is hoped that the brief outline given of some salient features of man's pre-historic and historic activities will serve as a useful guide to those who wish to take their first steps towards the goal of understanding man and his life styles as completely as possible.

CHAPTER 1

Human Origins and Early Migrations

It is now widely believed that man emerged from a pre-human primate background in Africa and that this was a unique event. Few would today accept the "hologenetic" theory of human origins suggesting that mankind originated sporadically and perhaps simultaneously in many different areas. In the past there were many speculations regarding the location of the area in which the emergence of man occurred. Both southern Asia and Africa have been posited but, particularly in view of the numerous, chronologically determinable fossil finds in Africa in recent years, there is now little doubt but that this latter continent, and perhaps particularly its eastern and southern areas, saw the remarkable transition from non-human creatures to the South African Ape-men or Australopithecinae, and to man proper.

This initial emergence during the Pleistocene Period is in itself a demonstration of a unique adaptability in the creatures involved. The Pleistocene Period is now estimated to be from 2 to 3 million years long, including a protracted earlier portion known as the Villafranchian, which was formerly assigned to the Pliocene (Tertiary). However, the International Geological Congress meeting in London in 1948 assimilated the Villafranchian into the Pleistocene because its deposits contain fossil remains of true horses, cattle, elephants and camels. During the Pleistocene many parts of the world, including Europe, where much of the chronology was initially established, experienced recurring intrusions of colder, glacial, conditions, with equally distinct long warm intervals. With the periodic desiccation of forested regions in Africa, a process equated in time with the glacial events in Europe during the Pleistocene period, many of the ecological niches which favoured the existence of arboreal creatures disappeared. It is likely

1

that many such animals became extinct; others might well have retreated into the diminished forested regions where they became further specialized and where their descendants the African Apes yet live. Other, perhaps numerous, primates competed with one another for the ecological niches increasingly available on the fringes of the primary forest zones and on the nearby grasslands. The competition may well have been very severe in these circumstances and groups which could swiftly adapt themselves to these conditions, involving living on the ground and away from close proximity to trees must have been very remarkable creatures. In terms of their morphological or physical attributes they were virtually defenceless. They were not particularly fleet-footed; they had no body armour or similar means of defence; they had small teeth, of little use either for defensive or aggressive purposes. Yet they must have been able to compete successfully with large predators and with many herbivores in the challenging new environment in which they lived. This was possible because they had an enhanced awareness of the world about them; they were increasingly able to foresee and to forecast all manner of eventualities, all because they were equipped with a relatively large brain, certainly large enough to enable them to supplement nature's endowments with tools which they were able to conceptualize and to manufacture according to set and regular patterns. Conceptualization involves intelligence, as does the manufacturing, but it also implies certain zoological modifications including the emancipation of the hand from its previous function as a mere supporter of the body to a delicate, precisely manipulated means of creating from natural objects those artifacts which the mind envisaged. These tools, the hallmark of mankind, appeared as long ago as 2 million years and being frequently made of durable stones, they have remained as unquestionable evidence of the presence of the now extinct forms of humanity which created them. It is extremely likely that wood, antler and bone tools were also manufactured in large quantities but the less durable nature of these substances makes it necessary for us to rely upon stone tools as the prime evidence of the early cultures of man.

These very early men or near-men, such as were found in the Olduvai Gorge in Tanzania, were organized into social groupings of some kind. Dwelling sites or "floors" have been found in the Pleistocene

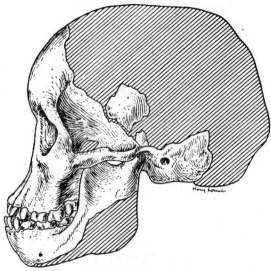

Australopithecus africanus

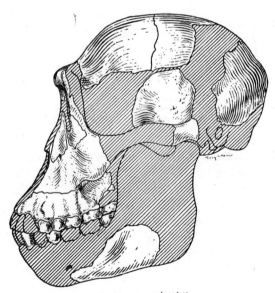

Australopithecus robustus

Fig. 1. Australopithecinae (after Ashley Montagu, 1951).

deposits there. It is virtually certain that effective means of communicating with one another existed among these humans and near humans (or hominids as they are frequently styled). The Australopithecinae were no more than 140cm tall and probably weighed some 27–30 kg at most. Sexual dimorphism, that is differences in size and in proportions between the sexes, was not pronounced in these essentially

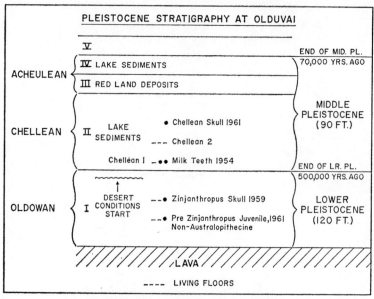

FIG. 2. Pleistocene stratigraphy at Olduvai.

hominid creatures. The brain was small, as in apes, varying from 400 to 700 cm³, but it is quite certain that their behavioural patterns were not ape-like. Having left the forested habitats which virtually every other primate to this day prefers, these bipedal creatures moved about much as we do. This is clearly evidenced by their bony remains, especially of the foot, pelvis, spine and cranium which in each case are specially adapted for bipedal, erect, locomotion. These bipeds were, in certain behavioural respects, very like the hunters and gatherers of today. At Olduvai there are complete living floors and the bony remains of animals found there and indeed elsewhere show that the Australopithecinae were successful hunters of all types of game animals.

They appear to have been able to use their hands and arms for clubbing and for throwing objects and, at Olduvai, they manufactured a great variety of tools both for cutting up game animals, once killed, and for making other tools, for preparing skins and for digging up roots. There is also evidence at Olduvai of a living structure, possibly a wind-break, used by the early hominids. Living hunters and gatherers at their encampments leave debris and objects lying around when they leave. By comparison with the quantities of material left behind at the Olduvai encampments it seems likely that a band was there composed of some dozen or so individuals staying in any one place for some days at a time. It is probable that the males hunted whilst the females foraged for food and small game which may have provided the greater part of the food supply. The males probably acted as protectors and directors of these small groups. In such bands therefore co-operative behaviour is essential and it appears unlikely that the males' role was that of pronounced "dominance" as is found in, for example, baboons in East Africa to this day. The absence of dimorphism—in body size and dentition—is important evidence that the Australopithecinae were hominid rather than pongid, since this is a feature of the hominids to this day. It must, of course, be remembered that the brain was at that time very small and that the Australopithecinae were far less intelligent than later hominids. As Pilbeam (1970) writes: "Richness and complexity of behaviour, particularly language, may well have been poor" (p. 164).

Early hominid life on the ground has been fully described by many writers, including Kurtén (1972, pp. 91 et seq.). Somewhat graphically he visualizes a hominid band trekking in search of new hunting grounds. Since they are walking bipedally they can see over the savannah grasses and they can keep a sharp look out for both game animals and enemies. At the approach of danger the band runs to the nearest tree(s), the slowest runner, lagging behind, possibly becoming a victim. In the absence of trees the hominids would hide or put up a fierce collective defence.

Such a group transports babies, food and weapons whilst a hunting party, mostly if not exclusively male, will only carry weapons. On sighting a small game animal one of the hunters will rush after it and catch it, the brief but violent exertion causing sweat droplets to glisten in his thin fur, efficiently dissipating body heat. There might well be selection against having a thick coating of fur and for having an increased number of sweat glands—a ground-living innovation. The animal captured is slit open, using teeth, fingers and sharp pieces of rock and once the flesh is eaten the pelt may be carried along, perhaps to be chewed upon later, if hungry. This in turn suggests a measure of forethought. A chewed skin is then made pliable and eventually conceptualized as a bag or a covering for the body during cold nights. Leather "curing" by chewing is in fact practised to this day by some human societies including the Eskimo.

Trekking in this way is difficult for children and for females carrying young and so the band may select a semi-permanent home in an appropriate area. Children and the adults caring for them may remain here whilst the hunting parties are foraging. In this way the family bond becomes important. The foraging parent must without fail perform the duty of bringing back food to the dependants. At a pre-hominid level only the mother–child bond is significant; now the additional bonds of father–child and perhaps most important, the sexual bonds of parents, evolve. Sexuality gradually pervades the life of the hominid, in contrast to its incidental role among other primates. The two-parent family became the fundamental nucleus of the population.

It is, however, incorrect to assume that the division of labour between the sexes was complete. Such complete division tends to produce great sexual dimorphism in size, the males being much larger than the females. Such dimorphism does not occur in the early hominids.

Territorial behaviour becomes increasingly important and complex and territorial units, hunting and home grounds, are guarded. Relationships with other groups range from peaceful coexistence to life and death struggles. Selection favours comradeship and loyalty to the group in face of external threats of all kinds. Kurtén (p. 94) suggests that the family forms a territorial sub-unit kept together by the family bond and that there is the seed of possible conflict between family and tribal loyalty. Rituals and taboos may have emerged as means of minimizing social disruption. "Cultural evolution is on its way, interdigitating with biological evolution."

The hands became free to manipulate weapons and other objects and they became progressively more skilful at satisfying the ever-growing curiosity of the brain. With increasing manual skill, the capacity of the brain is also augmented. Weapons and tools are fashioned and man the tool-maker comes into his own.

The ancient call system is superseded by true language, initially with a limited vocabulary. The utterance of sounds may be regarded as the essence of primate life and certainly the primates are the noisiest of mammals. Primatologists regard language not as the result of something radically new and exclusively human but

> Rather as a quantitative perfection of the highly specialized development of man's central nervous control of the anatomical speech apparatus in the larynx, tongue and lips. . . . As soon as the early hominids had ventured into open spaces, had begun to use and even make tools, and had co-operated in hunting, the total variety of all means of expression needed additions, which could only come from an increase in sounds, since the comparatively little changed anatomy had already been fully used for all possible gestures etc. . . . Gestures have always persisted in human evolution, but they have become over-shadowed by an infinitely greater variety of sounds in increasing numbers of combinations (Schultz, 1962).

Oakley and others have suggested that the early hominids may have depended primarily on gestures "mainly of mouth and hands, accompanied by cries and grunts to attract attention" and that speech may have been a comparatively late development (Oakley, 1951). If this were so then a non-hominid mode of communication would have persisted in the protocultural phase of hominid evolution. It is, however, very difficult to comprehend how a fully developed cultural adaptation could have existed without speech. If a speech community is one of the necessary conditions for the functioning of a typically human system of communication, then an organized social system is as necessary for human language as it is for a cultural mode of adaptation.

Hockett (1958) indicated that "Part of the problem of differentiating man from the other animals is the problem of describing how human language differs from any kind of communicative behaviour carried on by non-human or prehuman species." He identified seven key properties of the speech of *Homo sapiens* and compared them with the data available for non-human systems of communication. He showed that there was considerable overlap in terms of the properties considered though they did "not recur, as a whole set, in any known non-human communicative system". Hockett suggests a tentative evolutionary reconstruction. One of the key properties of a human system of communication is "cultural transmission" and this property is absent in the communication systems of the other primates. It is therefore chronologically highly significant. Learning and the social transmission of habits may well have existed at a very early stage in the development of the higher primates but the associated system of communication that prevailed may have operated without "cultural transmission".

> The significance of the fact that these earliest codes of communication did not function through learning and social transmission lies in the limitations this imposed upon the systems of social action developed in non-hominid and, perhaps, the earliest hominid groups. At the same time, these codes of communication, operating through the same sensory modes that appear at a later level may be considered prerequisite for the evolutionary development of a communication system characterized by the total assemblage of properties discussed by Hockett (Hallowell, 1962).

The systematic use of language and the large-scale manufacture of durable stone tools are the starting-point for a new type of evolution in which cultural factors are inextricably interwoven with the genetic. New modes of life opening up for the hominids could be fully exploited only by an increase in intelligence and only after the Australopithecine stage do we find a spectacular and rapid increase in brain size.

Kurtén (1972) is very much aware that the data and the ideas inferred from them in such theorizing are deductions which, with more knowledge, might appear quite inadequate. However, they show facets of social behaviour which, without such inference, could never be glimpsed.

Man is, above all, distinguished as the sole systematic tool-maker and hominid status is often conferred simply in terms of this unique capability. At all levels of the Lower Pleistocene Bed I at Olduvai Gorge there is unequivocal evidence of tool-making. Pebble-choppers, the most characteristic artefact found there, consist of smooth, waterborne cobblestones which have been crudely flaked by three or four strokes on two opposing faces of one end or one side, thus producing a chopping edge. The unworked, rounded butt fits into the palm of the hand. Lava pebble choppers abound in Bed I at Olduvai but spherical balls of quartzite, quartz scrapers, quartz flakes and crude hand axes also occur. It is interesting to note that the hand axes do not occur in the lower part of Bed I but they become increasingly frequent at the higher levels of Bed I and the lower levels of Bed II (Middle Pleistocene). It would appear that this new type of tool, very characteristic of the Middle Pleistocene cultures generally, was, as Napier (1971) puts it, in the "development" stage but not yet in "production" in Bed I at Olduvai Gorge. Craftsmanship in which manual delicacy and precision play a large part was generally absent from the Olduvai (Bed I) cultures. None the less neither the pebble tools nor any of the other variants can be regarded as mere accidents. Their constancy of shape indicates that an industry had been developed in which tradition and learning were playing their part. A tool-making industry indicates the "culturization" of tool-making. The archaeological characteristic of a tool-making culture is the manufacture of tools to a set and regular pattern. Cultural tool-making contains as an essential ingredient the element of tradition by which skill is transmitted from one generation to another. It is entirely feasible that the evolution of cultural tool-making, the final stage of the tool-making saga, followed close upon the heels of the evolution of speech and language.

Napier (1971) rightly points out that speech is not the only way by which information can be transmitted from one individual to another. Learning by precept and example would be an entirely feasible means by which one hominid might teach another as simple an activity as pebble tool-making. "It has never seemed to me that lack of language and speech would be any bar to the development of simple cultural traditions, although it has for long been explicit that speech and culture as so reciprocally linked that one is not possible without the other." Washburn (1960) suggests that "Language may have appeared together with fine tools, fire and the complex hunting of large-brained men of the middle Pleistocene . . .".

Technologically the Olduvai Bed I tool-making was very rudimentary. The succeeding hand-axe culture occurred in two phases: the older or Chellean, producing crude, roughly oval stone tools, and the more recent Acheulean culture, producing a much more delicately flaked, pear shaped stone, decorated by scalloping with sharp edges. The Olduvai-type pebble chopper was probably the cultural forerunner of the hand axe of Europe and Africa and of the crude chopper of the Far East.

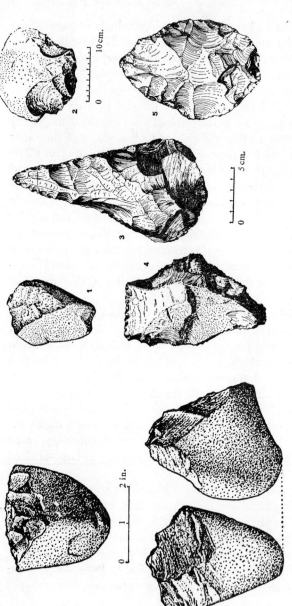

Lower Palaeolithic stone tools

1. Oldowan implement, Bed 1, Olduvai Gorge, Tanzania, East Africa
2. Choukoutienian chopper tool, Lower Cave, Peking, Peoples' Republic of China
3. Acheulean lanceolate hand axe or ficron, Swanscombe, Kent
4. Clactonian flake tool, Swanscombe, Kent
5. Acheulean hand axe, Swanscombe, Kent

After Day, 1965

Oldowan pebble-tools of lava from Bed 1, Olduvai Gorge

After Oakley, 1966

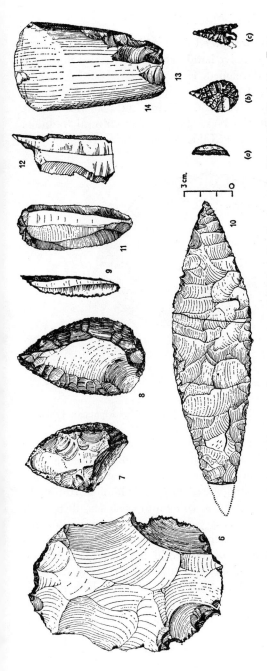

Middle and Upper Palaeolithic, and Neolithic stone tools

6. Levalloisian flake tool, Baker's Hole, Kent
   Drawn by courtesy of the Trustees of the British Museum
7. Mousterian side scraper
8. Mousterian point, Le Moustier, Dordogne, France
9. Gravettian backed blade, Les Roches, Sergeac, Dordogne, France
   Drawn by courtesy of the Trustees of the British Museum
10. Solutrean laurel-leaf blade, Solutré, Dordogne, France
    Drawn by courtesy of the Trustees of the British Museum
11. Magdalenian end scraper, La Madelaine, Dordogne, France
    Drawn by courtesy of the Trustees of the British Museum
12. Magdalenian burin, Dordogne, France
13. (*a*) Lunate microlith, Brakfontein, Cape Province, Republic of South Africa
    (*b*) British Neolithic leaf-shaped arrowhead
    (*c*) Neolithic tanged and barbed arrowhead, Fayum, Egypt
14. Neolithic polished flint axe-head, Thames Valley
    After Day, 1965

FIG. 3. Stone tools from various prehistoric cultures (after Oakley, 1966 and Day, 1965).

The pebble-chopper culture spread from Africa and, in north-west Eurasia, developed into successive hand-axe cultures, whilst in the Far East the chopper culture developed. Hand axes have not been found in Asia further east than India and choppers, like those found at Choukoutien, the home of the Middle Pleistocene men near Pekin, have never been found in the West. Two distinct cultural traditions may therefore be posited for the Middle Pleistocene.

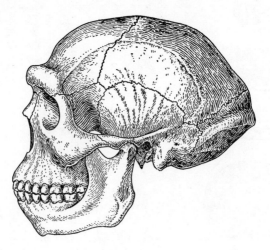

Fig. 4. *Homo erectus*—Middle Pleistocene man (after Ashley Montagu, 1951).

Thus it would seem that a rudimentary social organization and the transmission of cultural data by verbal communication is a very ancient feature of hominid life and indeed is frequently taken as the basic means of defining hominid status. Once this hominid threshold had been crossed and man *per se* had come into existence, then, with unquestioned and undisputed mastery over his animal competitors for foodstuffs and living space in eastern Africa, he seems very swiftly to have migrated to many parts of the Old World, so that remains of very early forms of man have been found in southern Asia, in Africa itself, in Europe and also in eastern Asia. Certainly there could have been no effective opposition to these early, migrating humans. Many reasons have been propounded to explain why these migrations should in fact have occurred at all, in view of the distinct possibility that man, like so many creatures, was partly controlled by a "territorial imperative" which tied him thereby to a limited part of the earth's surface. Local natural calamities, population increases as a consequence of the much more plentiful and assured food supplies available by using the new tool assemblages, intergroup difficulties and the attractiveness of new areas briefly seen during hunting trips may each, among other factors, partly account for what really amounts to an extraordinary phenomenon of rapid migration which by the end of the Middle Pleistocene period saw such a widespread distribution of the early form of man known as *Homo erectus.*

The close of the Middle Pleistocene was marked by the onset of desiccation in many areas which had nurtured hand-axe industries and their makers. Much of the Sahara became desert and this major ecological disturbance destroyed the cultural homogeneity which had characterized the whole of Africa and contiguous areas of Europe and Asia. North Africa became an outlier of western Asia whilst the Congo and southern Africa generally became a backwater. In sub-Saharan Africa two cultural traditions coexisted in the Upper Pleistocene, in mutually exclusive areas. The Sangoan occurred in the Congo, Angola, the Zambezi and the Great Lakes regions; the Fauresmith on high ground in Kenya, the Orange Free State and Bechuanaland. Both were characterized by hand axes and faceted flakes struck from prepared cores but they differed in detail. Cultural continuity and lack of essential change seemed to be the keynote, as was the case also in eastern Asia. There the old chopping tool and flake traditions persisted, as with the Soan culture of northern India, without contributing anything essential to the course of world prehistory.

The Advanced Palaeolithic cultures developed and flourished in north-western parts of the Lower Palaeolithic world and it was upon these developments that the future of mankind was largely to depend. In this area, the cultures in existence at the onset of the last (Würm) glaciation were essentially Lower Palaeolithic in character and were associated with Neanderthaloid men. In many areas of western Europe this culture is described as Mousterian, named after the rock shelter of Le Moustier in the Dordogne valley of south-west France. The tool assemblage was very restricted, comprising scrapers and points made from flakes trimmed on one or both edges by secondary flaking and also including small triangular or heart-shaped hand axes. South of this area, in Palestine, Syria, Iraq and south-west Iran, and also in northern Africa, the industries had a Levalloisian character, differing in detail from the cognate industries further north.

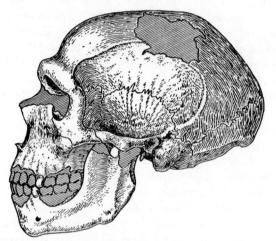

FIG. 5. Neanderthal man (after Ashley Montagu, 1951).

The Neanderthaloids frequently occupied caves, as on Mount Carmel, and bones preserved in these caves present full information about the animals which they hunted, the use they made of bone and related materials and the manner in which they disposed of their dead. They do not appear to have been more proficient hunters than their immediate forebears. It appears that no extended range of animals was hunted nor did the methods of hunting improve with time. Wooden spears, stone balls (bolas stones) and pit traps were used but there is a pronounced absence of specialized projectile-heads. Very little use was made of bone and related material in tool manufacture. It was later in the Palaeolithic period that men produced varied and beautiful antler, bone and ivory spear, harpoon and arrowheads, fish-hooks, a variety of other tools and objects for personal ornament. Again the Neanderthaloids showed no signs of having a developed aesthetic sense. Grahame Clark (1961) writes:

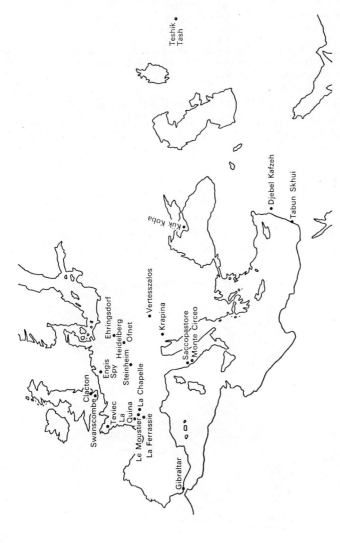

FIG. 6. Neanderthal sites in Europe and Western Asia (after Weiner, 1971).

Lower Palaeolithic man was capable of producing a limited range of tools with an astonishing economy of effort, and the perfection of form and degree of standardization that they achieved, often over great areas and despite wide variations in the qualities of the raw materials used, bear witness to firmness of intention and a definite sense of style; but as far as we know he practised no art—no sign of carving or engraving, for example, has been found among all the wealth of bone and antler from Mousterian and kindred sites; nor is there evidence of even so much as a single buried tooth to suggest that he fabricated ornaments to adorn his person.

However, Neanderthal Man extended the range of settlement well to the north of the frost-free zone to which most earlier men had confined themselves, and he did so during a period of glacial intensity. Parts of Central Asia were colonized, as evidenced by the remains at Teshik Tash in Uzbekistan, and even China was reached. During Würm I the Levalloiso Mousterian people occupied caves and utilized well-made flint scrapers to process animal skins into clothing. Their sometimes elaborate treatment of the dead, including ritualization, indicates that the Neanderthaloids had developed ideological concepts perhaps unexpected in view of their poorly developed material culture.

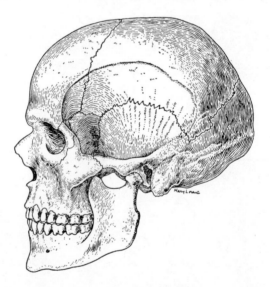

Fig. 7. Cromagnon man (after Ashley Montagu, 1951).

The Stone Age cultures which first developed between 30,000 and 40,000 years ago in Europe and western Asia are often referred to as Advanced Palaeolithic cultures, principally in view of their highly developed technological expertise. They were virtually confined to the more northerly parts of the Old World. To the south the Lower Palaeolithic cultures persisted though modified, until comparatively recent times and these areas, in Africa, India and south-east Asia, were by-passed by the main currents of creative change during the remainder of prehistoric times.

The men of the late or upper Pleistocene were physically and intellectually much as we are today. These Advanced Palaeolithic men were specialized hunters, using a variety of weapons, adorning their persons and practising an art replete with imaginative awareness and stylistically advanced creativity. Their technology was founded on stone (lithic) industries involving the production, by some kind of punch, of blades or flakes relatively narrow in proportion to their length and having fairly regular, parallel flake scars. Various types of blades were produced, each adapted to certain specialist functions including knife blades, projectile points, barbs, scrapers and burins the latter of the utmost importance in the working of bone and antler, as well as for engraving. The greatly increased utilization of antler and bone was a highly significant feature of the Advanced Palaeolithic industries which are, on the whole, far more diversified and highly specialized than the preceding cultures.

Grahame Clark (1961) gives the sequence of the Advanced Palaeolithic cultures established in south-western France.

TABLE 1. SIMPLIFIED SEQUENCE OF ADVANCED
PALAEOLITHIC CULTURES IN SOUTH-WESTERN FRANCE
(after Grahame Clark, 1961)

Radio-carbon dates B.C.	Cultures
15,000–8000	Magdalenian
18,000–15,000	Solutrean
22,000–18,000	Gravettian (Upper Perigordian)
28,500–22,000	Aurignacian
32,000–28,500	Chatelperronian (Lower Perigordian)

These cultures indicate a progressive development of technological skills and artistic creativity through time, each characterized by a unique assemblage of tools and other accomplishments. That of the Magdalenians, a culture which developed from the Gravettian and which flourished in a limited territory from south-west Germany, across France to eastern Spain, is perhaps the most famous and will be briefly characterized. This culture is notable for its marked development of the use of bone and especially of antler for the manufacture of a great variety of objects—weapons, implements and items for personal adornment. Moreover, both cave art and the embellishment of smaller objects were carried to a new peak of sophistication. The cave art of the Solutreo-Magdalenians was marked by attempts to suggest fullness. Figures were thrown into apparent relief by cutting away the surrounding rock or else by a series of fine hatching. In painting the artists attained to polychrome representations outlined in black, as at Altamira and Font de Gaume, before relapsing at the end of the Pleistocene into small red drawings. The bone and antler work likewise is very remarkable particularly the reindeer-antler spear-throwers which characterize the middle phases of the culture. These highly functional objects were enriched by representations of horses, ibex, bison and other animals in full or partial relief. Clark (1961) writes: "Altogether the art of this last phase of the Upper Palaeolithic in western Europe reflects the apogee of an advanced hunting culture operating in conditions that must have been highly congenial and productive of leisure."

Some 10,000 years ago Neothermal, that is, much warmer conditions of climate, began, and this onset markedly influenced the course of prehistoric events. The advanced Upper Palaeolithic people occupying regions subject to Late Glacial climates were especially affected. Ecological changes there were so great and so sudden that the whole balance of the societies involved was changed and major cultural re-adjustments were required, re-adjustments which distinguished the new Mesolithic from the preceding Advanced Palaeolithic societies. The distinction between the Advanced Palaeolithic and the following Epi-Palaeolithic (Mesolithic) cultures is less clear in areas further to the south which witnessed no such abrupt climatic changes as the more northerly areas.

All experts would agree that hunting was a part of the social adaptation of all populations of the genus *Homo* until very recently. Less than

1 per cent of the period of human existence has been dominated by agriculture. A particular combination of circumstances was required before mankind could establish an economy based upon food production, as in farming, in place of the pre-existing economy based upon the food extraction of the hunters and gatherers. When hunting and the way of life of successive populations of the genus *Homo* are considered it must be borne in mind that there was major technical and biological progress during this period of time of some half million or more years. However, for the present purpose, it is necessary to focus attention upon the cultural modifications which occurred during the 10,000 to 15,000 years before agriculture. No convenient term exists for this period which covers the very late Palaeolithic and the Mesolithic period but its importance is considerable. Thus during most of human history bodies of water constituted major physical and psychological barriers. There was a marked inability to cope with water, recorded archaeologically by the absence of remains of fish, shellfish or any object requiring going deeply into water, or of the use of boats. The resources of river and sea were first utilized on any significant scale during this late pre-agricultural phase as is witnessed by the huge shellfish middens of the period.

Again there was great technical progress during the late pre-agriculture period. The variety of stone tools used became much greater and bows and arrows, grinding stones, boats, much more advanced houses and even villages, sledges and the domestic cat and dog all appear. The technology of all the living hunters belongs to this late Mesolithic era at the earliest and many have cultural elements derived from agricultural and metal-using peoples. The occasional high population densities of hunters are based upon this very late and modified extension of the hunting and gathering economy. Good examples which persisted until the twentieth century occur among the tribes of the north-west coast of North America including the Haida and the Kwakiutl. These communities utilized polished stone axes for woodworking and greatly relied upon the products of rivers and sea.

The presence of the dog is a good indicator of the late pre-agricultural period. Dogs were of great importance in hunting, as they are today, among the Bushmen for example. Thus with the acquisition of dogs, bows and boats, hunting became much more complex in the few thousand years before agriculture.

Again the gathering and the preparing of food became far more complex during this period. Man gathers a great variety of items which cannot be digested without soaking, boiling, grinding or otherwise preparing in some manner. Seeds may well have constituted a very important factor in human diet both because they were abundant and because they could readily be stored. Grinding stones appear before agriculture and it may well be that grinding and boiling may have been the necessary pre-conditions to the discovery of agriculture. Washburn and Lancaster (in Washburn and Jay, 1968) have written:

> We think that the main conclusions, based on the archaeological record, ecological considerations, and the ethnology of the surviving hunter-gatherers, will be sustained. In the last few thousand years before agriculture, both hunting and gathering became much more complex. This final adaptation, including the use of products of river and sea and the grinding and cooking of otherwise inedible seeds and nuts, was world-wide, laid the basis for the discovery of agriculture, and was much more effective and diversified than the previously existing hunting and gathering adaptations.

Most authorities would agree that the initial transition from a modified hunting and gathering economy to an economy based on the cultivation of crops and domesticated animals—the so-called Neolithic Revolution—occurred in the Middle East. Carl O. Sauer (1969) has argued that south-east Asia is the "cradle of earliest agriculture". This area meets

> The requirements of high physical and organic diversity, of mild climate with reversed monsoons giving abundant rainy and dry periods, of many waters inviting to fishing, of location at the hub of the Old World for communication by water or by land. No other area is equally well situated or equally well furnished for the rise of a fishing-farming culture (Sauer, 1969).

He attempts to show that the "Farming culture in origin is tied to fishing in this area, that the earliest and most literally domestic animals originated here, and that this is the world's major centre of planting techniques and of amelioration of plants by vegetative reproduction." However, it is overwhelmingly likely that a food-gathering economy was initially replaced by one of food producing from the eighth millennium B.C. onwards in south-west Asia. In this region, extending from Palestine and Syria to the Zagros Mountains both wheat and barley grow wild and here also lived the wild ancestors of dogs, goats, sheep, cattle and pigs. Man was at last freed of the vicissitudes of hunting. In this radically new phase in human existence men learned to polish stone implements, to live in houses grouped together in villages, to raise crops, store food, domesticate animals, make pottery and weave cloth. However, this whole complex was not on all occasions adopted as a single unit. Thus at Tell Murebat, an ancient village near the river Euphrates in Syria, the community established there 9500 years ago lived in closely crowded houses which were built at a time when the inhabitants were still dependent upon game animals as their primary food supply. The grains which were used to supplement their diet were wild varieties. With regard to planting the term "vegeculture" has been used for the first stage since "fields" (*ager*: agriculture) are not implied until the socio-cultural level reached a high degree of intensification. Sauer believes that vegeculture began in south-east Asia and its origins in Mexico are perhaps as ancient as in the Old World.

The villages in the Middle East where agriculture was first practised were located within or at the periphery of the woodland belt extending from Greece to Cyprus, Turkey, Palestine, Iraq and the Persian Gulf. Three major agricultural settlements occur in the east of this region—Jarmo, Zawi Chemi Shanidar, and Karim Shahir—all in pleasant areas with mild weather, having alternating wet and dry seasons, varied woodland, hills and valleys, streams and springs, alluvial stretches and rock shelters in cliffs. The early sites in Palestine, however, have poorer natural surroundings and climate. Initially the Natufians of the Palestine region were essentially food-gatherers although they had knowledge of the cultivation of grain. Most of their food was obtained by fishing and hunting. The population was growing rapidly and harpooning fish and hunting gazelle with dogs did not produce a sufficiently steady food supply. These Natufians were camping, in small numbers, near the Jericho spring as early as 7800 B.C., as is indicated by their remains at the base of the tell* there. There followed

---

* The term "tell" is derived from the Babylonian *tillu*, "ruin heap". Generally speaking tells now appear as truncated cones composed of the accumulated debris, especially ruined and destroyed buildings, of groups who successively occupied the site. The depth of the tell debris at Jericho is approximately 20 metres and this figure is greatly exceeded at sites such as Susa in Mesopotamia. The terms *hüyük* and *tepe* are synonyms of "tell".

a period often termed proto-Neolithic in which it appears that the scale of domestication of crops and animals became increasingly greater but during which pottery was not manufactured. The whole Neolithic complex was established during the seventh millennium B.C.

This revolutionary change from hunting to farming laid the foundations of a civilized way of life. Prior to this period communities had been very much restricted by the numbers of the game animals and the quantities of edible plants available. It now became possible to plant larger quantities of seeds, to cultivate greater areas of land and to breed more livestock, as population numbers increased. Families joined together for communal food production and for defence. Greater economic production allowed a measure of security and leisure during which the arts of civilization might be developed. With food surpluses accumulated, specialized craftsmen could be supported whilst they devoted much of their time and energy to the manufacture of tools, pottery, clothing and buildings. Settlements near perennial sources of water were permanent. In less-favoured areas shifting hoe-cultivation was practised, the cultivators moving on once the land was exhausted or infected with weeds beyond their control. The Neolithic farmers who moved into Europe appear to have practised this latter type of cultivation.

Before considering the spread of the Neolithic communities into Europe, it is of interest to consider the natural species of plants and animals which, occurring naturally in parts of the Middle East, allowed the possibility of domestication to be realized there. Wheat and barley were fundamental to the new economy in the Middle East. Their grains are highly nutritious and easily stored, the return is high and the labour involved is seasonal allowing leisure for other occupations. Deliberate selection of the best seed for sowing and accidental crossing of available varieties produced grains with seeds very much larger than the seeds of wild grasses.

It should be emphasized that these wild forms of wheat and barley are common plants in their natural habitats, frequently covering extensive tracts of territory. They are important constituents of the sub-Mediterranean oak park-forest belt extending around the Syrian desert to the Euphrates basin. Zohary (in Ucko and Dimbleby, 1969) reports that in the Upper Jordan Basin, for example, on uncultivated slopes "natural fields of these wild cereals extend over many kilometres. In their growth and total mass these wild fields of wheat, barley and oats are not inferior to their cultivated counterparts. These robust wild forms can be favourably compared with their cultivated relatives in grain production also."

One very important Middle Eastern wild wheat is *Triticum boeoticum* or *T. aegilopoides* and this probably gave rise to Einkorn, *T. monococcum*, in which the ear of corn shattered less readily and so was easier to harvest. Ears of wild cereal disarticulate as soon as they mature and the process may be very abrupt in the dry, hot weather experienced at the end of the growing season in the Middle East. Wild cereal fields may shed their fruit and become barren dry stalks in a week or two, and therefore the effective harvesting period is very short. It is even shorter during the not infrequent extremely dry, warm spells sometimes

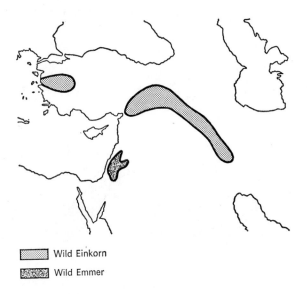

▓▓▓ Wild Einkorn

▓▓▓ Wild Emmer

Fig. 8. Distribution of Wild Emmer (*Triticum dicoccoides*) and of Wild Einkorn (*T. boeoticum*) (after Zohary in Ucko and Dimbleby, 1969).

referred to as the khamsin. Einkorn was grown during the early Neolithic and the first farmers introduced it into Europe but it is no longer
cultivated except in a few remote mountainous regions. *T. dicoccoides* is
closely related to the cultivated wheat, Emmer. This wheat was grown
in many parts of the Middle East during the early Neolithic, especially
in Egypt, and it was also extensively cultivated in Europe persisting in
parts there until well into the Christian era.

The Bread Wheat, *T. aestivum,* was unimportant until the Iron Age.
It is thought to have been derived from the Emmer group of wheats by
hybridization with a grass, Aegilops.

Wild barley grows in many parts of the Middle East and in a variety
of ecological conditions whilst wild barley and both varieties of wild
wheat grow in parts of Syria. The cultivation of barley occurs as early
as that of wheat. Two major types of barley are known, referred to as
two-row and six-row barley. The two-row barleys are represented by
Hordeum spontaneum, which grows wild in the Middle East and by *H.
distichum,* known only in cultivation. *H. agriocrithon,* the wild six-row
form, was first discovered in eastern Tibet but it has also been identified

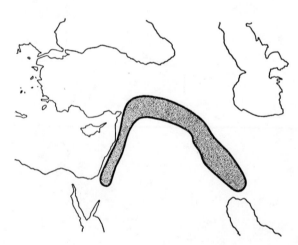

FIG. 9. Distribution of wild barley (*Hordeum spontaneum*) (after Zohary in Ucko
and Dimbleby, 1969).

in Palestine. The cultivated forms include *H. hexastichum* and *H. tetrastichum*. Six-row barley is more common at most early Neolithic sites though only two-row barley was found at Jarmo. Six-row barley was extensively cultivated in late Neolithic Europe but at present it is only grown in a few Alpine areas and sporadically elsewhere in Europe.

Other important cultivated crops in various parts of the world during the Neolithic included millet, sorghums, oats, rye, rice and maize, together with leguminous plants (peas, beans and lentils), oil-producing plants (olives, sesame and flax) and fruit trees.

The domestication of goats, sheep and cattle almost certainly first occurred in the Middle East where their wild ancestors still live. Apart from the dog, goats and sheep were the first domesticated animals and they were kept from the very beginning of the Middle Eastern Neolithic. Both pigs and cattle were domesticated a little later. Thus mixed farming began early in the Neolithic as the evidence from Jarmo, for example, clearly indicates.

Sonia Cole (1959) writes: "Animals were first valued for their meat and hides; then, as they became more docile, they would have

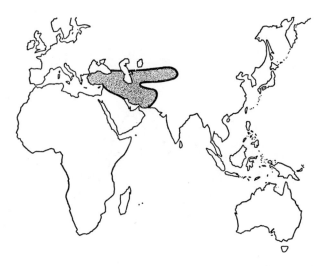

Fig. 10. Distribution of the wild goat (*Capra*) (after Cole, 1959).

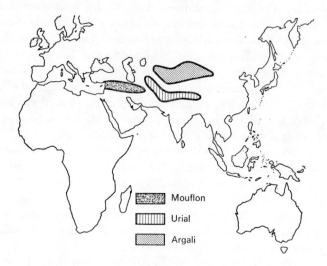

Fig. 11. Distribution of the wild sheep (*Ovis*) (after Cole, 1959).

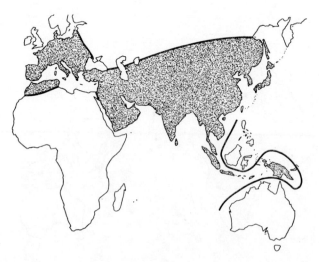

Fig. 12. Distribution of the wild pig (*Sus scrofa scrofa*) (after Cole, 1959).

been milked and finally they were used as pack animals. By killing off the wildest rams and bulls and preserving the more amenable, selective breeding would have begun."

Evidence for domesticated goats is first known from the pre-pottery Neolithic levels at Jericho and Jarmo, the former dated before 6000 B.C. These goats were derived from the bezoar, *Capra aegagrus*, which yet lives wild in mountainous areas of south-west Asia. The pre-pottery levels at Jarmo also contain remains of domesticated sheep but this is not so at Jericho. Domesticated sheep are derived from one or more of the three wild species native to Eurasia: the mouflon, urial and argali. Varieties of mouflon occur both in Europe and Asia and it is the descendants of the Asian variety, *Ovis orientalis*, whose remains are found in the early Neolithic deposits at Jarmo. In Britain, the Soay sheep is thought to be descended from the European mouflon *Ovis musimon*.

Neolithic farmers introduced a breed derived from the urial into Europe, from Asia and this Turbay sheep still survives in parts of the continent. Moreover, Merino and Norfolk Black Face sheep are considered to be of urial strain.

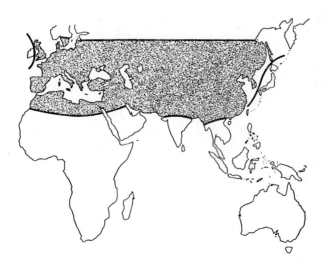

Fig. 13. Distribution of the wild aurochs (*Bos primigenius*) (after Cole, 1959).

The argali, *O. ammon*, is found in central Asia but apart from local contributions in that area it was unimportant as a forerunner of domesticated types of sheep.

The common wild boar, *Sus scrofa scrofa* gave rise to the domesticated pig and remains are known from pre-pottery Neolithic deposits at Jarmo. However, modern breeds are partly derived from *S. scrofa vittatus*, indigenous to south-east Asia. This latter sub-species was the only animal domesticated by the Neolithic farmers in China. The Chinese breed appears largely to have replaced the European breeds derived from *S. scrofa scrofa* during the eighteenth century A.D.

Wild aurochs or urus (*Bos primigenius*) gave rise to domesticated cattle probably about 4000 B.C. and again in the Middle East. These domesticated cattle were introduced into Europe by Neolithic farmers via the Danube basin.

The transition from a pre-agricultural to an agricultural way of life can not now be regarded as a single "revolutionary" step. It is evident that animal domestication and the beginnings of cultivation were slow and complex processes. These involved varied and gradual adjustments between man and the land over long periods of time and in many different environments. The Neolithic way of life was carried from the Middle East to many other parts of the world by migration and by the diffusion of techniques and ideas. In Europe the first Neolithic farmers appeared in Greece and areas to the north in the Balkans. Ammerman and Cavalli-Sforza (1971) have measured the rate of spread or diffusion. No serious claims for local domestication of either wheat or barley in Europe have been put forward and "Cereals which had reached northern Europe by 3000 B.C. provide almost a classic case of the diffusion of plants to a new area."

Early established patterns of migration have continued ever since among men, increasing in size, scope and complexity during the more recent centuries of human history. Migrations have presumably always been more pronounced features in some areas than in others, so that, by the beginning of recent times, some lands had witnessed a continuous cross-fertilization by diverse human groups over many millennia. Other areas have remained as stagnant backwaters with very few experiences of incursions of this kind. Thus while much of European and Middle Eastern history is a tale of continuous movements of peoples, the Khoisan (Bushmen and Hottentots) peoples of southern Africa have survived little changed by such factors until recently in many cases, since neither the Bantu nor the Europeans had reached these southern areas of Africa until a very few centuries ago.

The relative cultural levels attained by the world's peoples were manifestly and demonstrably extremely variable, as they still are to some extent. This cannot simply be attributed to any one cause. The notion put in the preceding paragraph that cross-fertilization might have led to some cultural advance is perhaps part, but only part, of the answer. Some have argued that the cause is to be sought in racial factors though it seems impossible to prove conclusively, if at all, that there are racial differences in mental potential and accomplishment. C. D. Darlington has defined intelligence as the ability of one man to

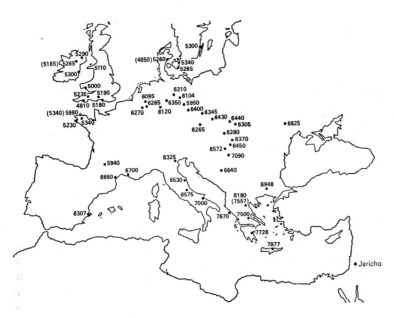

FIG. 14. The spread of early farming into Europe (after Ammerman and Cavalli-Sforza, 1971). (Dates are in years B.P.)

understand more than another and to understand it more quickly. Intelligence can therefore frequently be a matter of life and death. It is concerned with how the young learn and how the old survive and it involves families and groups as well as individuals. Thus questions of intelligence must be related to conditions of education, race and class if we are to secure useful answers to them: it is exceedingly difficult to separate the effects of economic status, educational opportunity and of inborn aptitude. Eysenck (1971) looked at evidence indicating the level of intelligence in various racial groups including Whites, Mexicans, Chinese and Negroes. Comparisons of these groups reveal their different reactions to education and economic opportunity and confirm their hereditary basis. Eysenck concludes that heredity accounts for some four-fifths of the difference between the White and Negro (Coloured) racial groups in the U.S.A. Many will find this an impalatable conclusion but the evidence put forward by Eysenck is difficult fully to refute. Eysenck himself states that neither the environmental nor the hereditarian arguments have been clearly established beyond doubt. Both explanations may be taken simply as theories but most certainly neither can nor should be ignored. Jensen and Eysenck throw doubt upon one of the corner-stones of liberal philosophy, that all men are intrinsically equal, as embodied in the 1951 UNESCO statement: "According to present knowledge there is no proof that the groups of mankind differ in their innate mental characteristics, whether in respect of intelligence or temperament. The scientific evidence indicates that the range of mental capacities in all ethnic groups is much the same." However, there is also no proof that innate mental differences do not exist.

It is impossible to say more at present than that science has not validly demonstrated any inherited mental differences between the races. Our recognition of races remains based upon physical or somatic features. That mental differences may parallel the physical differences is a possibility, but we do not yet possess adequate techniques for distinguishing between those mental characteristics which may be inborn or hereditary or racial, from those which are due to education and the environment generally" (Tobias, 1961).

Eysenck suggests the possibility that in the days of the slave raids the brighter individuals in African tribes might, because of their relatively high intelligence, have escaped. The less-intelligent individuals were caught and therefore the gene pool of those slaves taken to America would have been depleted of many high I.Q. genes. Again tribal chiefs in Africa may have sold into slavery many of their less-intelligent followers. Once in America, the more intelligent slaves might have been the most recalcitrant and the most prone to attempt escape and they may well have suffered appallingly as a result. Intelligence in the conditions of slavery was in fact counter-selective. Therefore the American Negro is a selected sub-sample where intelligence is at a disadvantage. "The inevitable outcome of such selection would of course be the creation of a gene pool lacking some of the genes making for higher intelligence." It is impossible to be certain of such counter-selective trends but the idea is of interest to those with an open mind on the matter. "All we can say is that even if there are no genetic differences in ability between negroes in general and whites, it is not impossible that American Negroes may be the descendants of a highly selected sample of African negroes less bright than the total group." Of other groups who migrated to the U.S.A., Eysenck suggests that the Irish, for example, probably showed the opposite tendency. In this instance it was the more intelligent members of the groups who emigrated, leaving their less-intelligent members behind.

Whichever view one takes of race differences in intelligence it is, however, true to say that many if not most of the great dramatic inventions among men have occurred only once and not more often in each case. With some possible exceptions, it seems very likely that the notions of domestication of animals and the cultivation of plants, the use of the wheel and of fire occurred firstly among certain groups of people in the Middle East and that knowledge of these revolutionary features spread thence to many other parts of the world. It is equally unlikely that these cultural features should have evolved separately, a second or third time, in each of the areas where they were ultimately formed. Redfield (1959) writes of the folk societies:

"The civilizations of the last five thousand years have destroyed them or have altered them with very small exception. One civilization that developed in Western Europe during very recent times indeed has reached into almost all of even the remote corners where they most successfully persisted in the primary condition. In this world-wide Western offensive against the rear-guard of the primitive societies, extermination or eviction or subjugation has been the rule and conversion the exception."

CHAPTER 2

The Races of Man

IN ADDITION to social and cultural diversity among human populations, great physical variability exists within the species *Homo sapiens* to which all living men belong. A certain awareness of the distinctive physical attributes of many human groups is of considerable antiquity. The people of the Classical World of the Mediterranean areas were very much aware of the different "barbarians" living in the lands to the north, in Europe, as well as of the black peoples of Africa. The recognition of such physical differences is very much part of the social scene in very many parts of the world today. Moreover, social patterns and forms of behaviour are frequently associated with these racial differences in people's minds. At a much later date racist doctrines implying the innate inferiority of certain races compared with others have thrived in certain "civilized" countries in twentieth-century Europe, but these are of no concern in the present study.

Physical anthropologists have devoted themselves to the problem of outlining on a scientific basis the evolution of man, the racial diversification and adaptability of the human species and also the distinctive physical attributes of the races of man today. These racial variables are simply seen as the result of man's biological adaptation to the ecological conditions and environmental stresses, both physical and human, in which he has evolved. Certain conditions have elicited a certain response in humans subjected to them; dissimilar circumstances have led to the emergence of other types of humanity. Thus whilst the peoples of central Asia and of Africa are obviously very dissimilar in the physical sense, such differences as they manifest are due to the quite different conditions in which the Mongols evolved in sub-Arctic conditions in central Asia, and the black Africans in tropical

32

Africa. The environmental stresses in these two areas evoked particular biological responses which we can still recognize in two of the major human races. No connotations of inferiority or of superiority in any sense, other than biological fitness to the circumstances in which they evolved and by now live, is implied.

There is much confusion over the meaning and the appropriate usage of the term "race" and the literature does not always help to clarify matters. Snyder (1962) observes of the term that

> It primarily denotes a biological category. Outside the field of biology the word tends to become utterly meaningless. Even under the loosest definition, race implies the existence of groups which have certain similarities in somatic characteristics which are perpetuated according to laws of biological inheritance (with a margin of individual variation).

Coon (1961) considers that "A race is, . . . , a group of people who possess the majority of their physical characteristics in common." Boyd (1950) maintains that races may validly be defined only by using physical characteristics whose precise mode of inheritance is known. Among these, the various blood groups are of paramount importance and upon this basis he proceeds to classify the world's peoples into major races, viz. Early European (Basque), European, Mongoloid, Negroid, American and Australian. Other classifications have been based upon stature, cephalic index (head breadth/head length $\times$ 100), hair form, pigmentation and a bewildering variety of other criteria.

As human groups adapt to environmental stresses, the successful modifications which occur must be in the genetic constitutions of the individuals in the groups, otherwise they are not transmitted to the ensuing generations and are lost. It is because of its enormous basic significance in this respect that in recent years physical anthropologists have concentrated so much effort upon comprehending the genetic composition of the world's peoples. Whilst head shapes undoubtedly vary from one people to another, it is with the present state of knowledge impossible to equate this diversity with clearly comprehended genetic factors. Head shapes vary a good deal as a result of artificial moulding of the head among other things and by no means exclusively because of genetic factors.

The blood groups, the haemoglobins and a whole range of other factors are directly controlled by fairly simple and clearly understood genetic factors or genes. Moreover, the races of man display great diversity in the frequencies with which the various genes occur among them. Few genes are the exclusive property of a single race, though a few instances do exist. It is far more usual for the differences to occur in the relative frequencies of the genes in these populations. These comprehended genetic systems provide an objective, increasingly respected means of considering, describing and analysing the racial diversity of man today, and, by various inferences, in the past also.

The first discovered and perhaps the best known of the blood-group systems is the ABO classification. This depends upon the inheritance of two genes in each individual from the genes present in the parents. Of the three genes, A, B and O, each individual has two, giving the following possible gene combinations or genotypes: AA, AO, BB, BO, AB and OO. With current blood-grouping procedures the presence of the O gene cannot be demonstrated in the presence of the so-called dominant A and B genes and thus there are only four recognizable blood-group types, or phenotypes: A, B, AB and O. Each phenotype is characterized by the presence of the appropriate blood-group substances on the red cells of the blood and in each case there are complementary antibodies present in the serum of the blood. The result is that only certain admixtures of blood types are possible in transfusion since various antibodies react with the blood-group substances or antigens.

However, from an anthropological viewpoint the most interesting matter is that the distribution of the A, B and O genes is extremely variable among the world's peoples (Figs. 15 and 16, Table 2). Thus the A and B genes are on the whole most frequent in continental areas whilst the O gene occurs very frequently in marginal areas such as far north-western Europe. The B gene is most prevalent in the Mongoloid peoples of central Asia whilst it does not occur at all among the aboriginal peoples of America, other than the Eskimo, nor does it occur except very rarely in Australia and then only in the extreme north, nor does it occur among the Basques other than with very low incidence.

Dr Kopeć has analysed over half a million blood-group record cards from all parts of the United Kingdom and her results for the ABO blood-group system show systematic and pronounced variation from

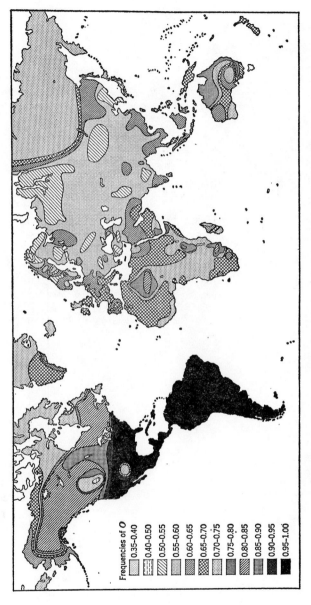

Fig. 15. The distribution in aboriginal populations of allele O of the ABO blood-group system (after Buettner-Janusch, 1966).

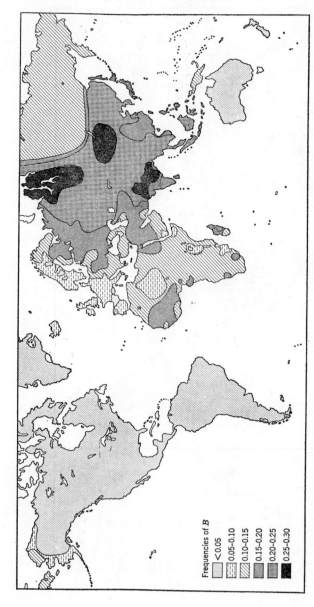

Fig. 16. The distribution in aboriginal populations of allele B of the ABO blood-group system (after Buettner-Janusch, 1966).

TABLE 2. DISTRIBUTION OF THE ABO BLOOD GROUPS

Population	Number	Percentage			
		O	A	B	AB
English (London)	422	47.9	42.4	8.3	1.4
Iceland	800	55.7	32.1	9.6	2.6
Basques (San Sebastian)	91	57.2	41.7	1.1	0.0
Germans (Berlin)	39,174	36.5	42.5	14.5	6.5
Ukranians (Kharkov)	310	36.4	38.4	21.6	3.6
Kirghiz (USSR)	500	31.6	27.4	32.2	8.8
Chinese (Pekin)	1000	30.7	25.1	34.2	10.0
Buriats (Irkutsk)	1320	32.4	20.2	39.2	8.2
Melanesians (New Guinea)	500	37.6	44.4	13.2	4.8
Polynesians (Hawaii)	413	36.5	60.8	2.2	0.5
Australian Aborigines (W. Australia)	243	48.1	51.9	0.0	0.0
Eskimo	484	41.1	53.8	3.5	1.4
N. American Indians (Utes, Montana)	138	97.4	2.6	0.0	0.0
N. American Indians (Navaho, New Mexico)	359	77.7	22.5	0.0	0.0
S. American Indians (Toba, Argentina)	194	98.5	1.5	0.0	0.0
Asiatic Indians (Bengal)	160	32.5	20.0	39.4	8.1
Arabs (Rwala, Syria)	208	43.3	22.1	30.3	4.3
Turks (Istanbul)	500	33.8	42.6	14.8	8.8
Egyptians (Cairo)	502	27.3	38.5	25.5	8.8
Ganda (Uganda Bantu)	450	68.7	18.7	12.0	0.7
Kikuyu (Kenya, Bantu)	449	60.4	18.7	19.8	1.1
Masai (Kenya Nilo Hamites)	233	48.1	20.2	30.5	1.3
Twa (Pygmies)	1000	71.5	14.5	12.1	1.9
Nn. Bushmen (South West Africa)	446	56.1	33.9	8.5	1.6
Hottentot (Korana, South Africa)	174	26.4	44.8	24.7	4.0

area to area within the country (Figs. 17, 18 and 19) despite the scale of the recent intense migration. Very different populations, in terms of the ABO blood-group system, occur to north and south of an east–west line running across northern England. Dr. Kopeć (1970) writes:

> The southern boundary of area 2 (35.56 for A, 50.74 for O) is the only line which marks a division for all three phenotypes, yet I think that it is only for A that the whole length of the line makes a sharp transition (from 35.56 to 39.65). Its western part determined a strong decrease of B + AB making the change of O

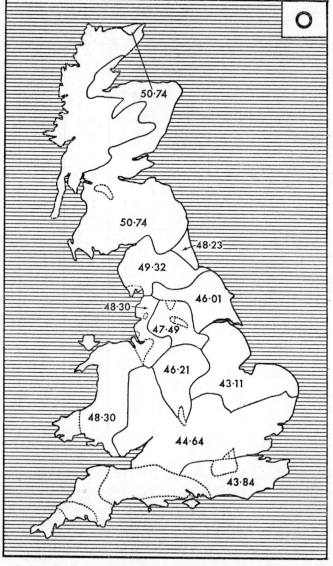

Fig. 17. The distribution of blood group O in England, Wales and Scotland (after Kopeć, 1970).

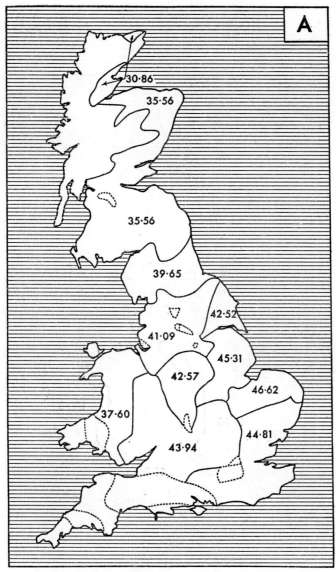

Fig. 18. The distribution of blood group A in England, Wales and Scotland (after Kopeć, 1970).

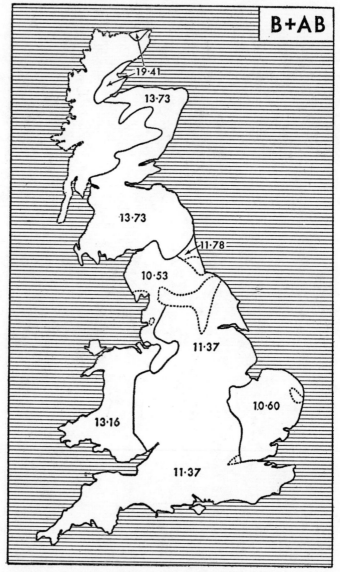

Fig. 19. The distribution of blood group B + AB in England, Wales and Scotland (after Kopeć, 1970).

less marked. This decrease was less definite in its eastern part so that the corresponding decrease of O is greater, but even there I am hesitant for O as I have been for B + AB and would place the really strong decrease of O further south, on the line between 49.32 and 46.01.

In general terms Kopeć showed that in Britain there is an increase in the frequency of the O gene northwards and westwards from southeast England, with a complementary decrease in the gene A frequency in the same direction. The B gene appears to be more frequent in the Celtic areas than in other parts of the country. Regional variation of this kind within the United Kingdom is geographically meaningful; the patterns as mapped do not simply indicate random fluctuations from place to place, and as indicated previously, dramatic changes of frequencies occur along clearly demarcated lines. Marked regional variability of the ABO genes is not due to random factors but due to a complex interplay of the genetic composition of populations and the environmental circumstances in which they live. Thus the various ABO genotypes are thought to be differentially susceptible to diseases such as plague and smallpox, and conditions such as duodenal ulceration would appear to affect individuals of certain ABO blood groups more frequently than others.

In the past, plague constituted a devastating destroyer of human life: there are still endemic foci in Central Asia, Iraq, south-west Arabia and Uganda. It is caused by a bacillus, *Pasturella pestis*, which produces an antigen in certain respects similar to the H substance or antigen of the blood group O. The H substance occurs, to a lesser degree, in individuals of blood group A_2.* It has been posited but not yet proven that individuals of blood types OO, A_2O and A_2A_2 are particularly susceptible to plague since they do not carry anti H antibodies in their sera. Thus populations long subject to plague should contain high frequencies of the blood groups which do have anti-H, namely, A_1, B and A_1B and this appears to be so. Not only is the theory logical but the geographical association is also close.

Smallpox, caused by the virus *Variola*, originated in Asia and was transported outwards by groups such as the Crusaders to Europe, and

---

* The blood group A may be further subdivided into the categories A_1 and A_2, the former being by far the more prevalent. The A_2 variety is virtually confined to European populations.

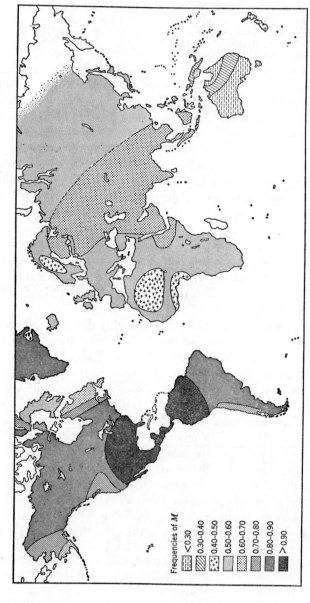

Fig. 20. The distribution in aboriginal populations of the allele M of the MNSs blood-group system (after Buettner-Janusch, 1966).

thence, at a later date to the New World. It has altered the distribution of humans in various parts of the world on a meaningful scale and it appears also to have affected the frequencies of the ABO and MN blood groups in certain populations.

Evidence for its possible association with the ABO blood groups is entirely geographical. In areas where smallpox is endemic, the O gene is at a minimum and both A and B gene frequencies are high. Its most deadly effects were upon populations which, before the appearance of the disease, were predominantly of blood-group O, as among the South American Indians and, to a lesser extent, those of North America also.

The relationship between smallpox and the MN blood-group system is evidenced by both geographical and clinical factors. In Old World areas with endemic smallpox M gene frequencies are considerably higher than the world average given by Mourant (1954). Among Amerindian tribes decimated by smallpox, the M gene frequency is very high, on occasion attaining a value of 90 per cent. Among Australian Aborigines and Papuans, which have not been exposed to smallpox on a large scale, the N gene frequencies usually range from 70 to 90 per cent (Table 3).

TABLE 3. DISTRIBUTION OF THE MN BLOOD GROUPS

Population	Number	Percentage		
		M	N	MN
English (London)	422	28.7	23.9	47.4
Basques (San Sebastian)	91	23.1	25.3	51.6
Germans (Berlin)	8144	29.7	19.6	50.7
Ukranians (Kharkov)	310	36.1	19.6	44.3
Chinese (Hong Kong)	1029	33.2	18.2	48.6
Papuans	200	7.0	69.0	24.0
Australian Aborigines (Queensland)	372	2.4	67.2	30.4
Eskimo	569	83.5	0.9	15.6
N. American Indians (Utes, Utah)	104	58.7	6.7	34.6
Arabs (Rwala, Syria)	208	57.5	5.8	36.7
Egyptians (Cairo)	502	27.8	23.3	48.9
Luo (Kenya Nilotes)	128	23.4	21.9	54.7
Valley Tonga (Zambia)	184	30.4	19.2	50.4
Bushmen (South-west Africa)	188	37.8	19.7	42.6
Hottentot (South-west Africa)	201	56.2	9.0	34.8

Clinical evidence from both Nigeria and Brazil indicates that individuals suffering from smallpox show the most severe symptoms if they are of group N and the least if they are of group M.

The frequency of blood-group O is higher—usually very much higher—in those suffering from duodenal ulcers than it is in the population at large. Conversely, blood-group A is less common among those affected. It is convenient to express the results in terms of the incidence of the disease in persons of one group relative to the incidence in the other group. This is done by simple cross multiplication. Thus in a London series those with duodenal ulcers number 535 of group O and 311 of group A whilst the population at large is randomly represented by samples of 4578 of group O and 4219 of group A. The expression

$$\frac{535 \times 4219}{311 \times 4578} = 1.59$$

indicates the interrelationships involved. In this series the incidence of duodenal ulceration in persons of group O is 1.59, compared with an incidence of 1, among persons of group A. Other series give the following results: London 1.54, Manchester 1.21, Newcastle upon Tyne 1.57, Oslo 1.56, Vienna 1.22, Iowa (Negroes) 1.32.

With stomach cancers the affected series show higher frequencies of group A than do the unaffected. However, the differences are, on average, smaller than for duodenal ulceration: London 1.20, Manchester 1.22, Newcastle upon Tyne 1.25, Copenhagen 1.30, Milan 1.28 and Sydney 1.06. For pernicious anaemia, the evidence for an excess of A is strong; duodenal ulceration is commoner in non-secretors of group-specific substances than among secretors; uterine cancers are commoner in females of group A than in those of group O. Thus selective pressures operate via diseases against certain of the blood groups. Yet, these persist in time since the selective pressures are counterbalanced by compensatory mechanisms and by mutations.

In large populations with conditions approximating to random mating (a theoretical concept rarely found in practice whereby an individual is considered to have an equal opportunity of marrying any one of the total possible mates available) gene frequencies attain a stable state; that is, their frequencies do not change from one generation to the next, unless different environmental stresses are introduced which may result in changes subsequently. For this reason it is valid to assume that populations displaying similar gene frequencies have a close affinity with one another even though they may be widely separated geographically. Such an assumption is in fact borne out by historical, cultural similar data.

Thus the gene frequencies of the present-day population of Iceland indicate the close affinity of the group with the people of Scandinavia and also reveal a sizeable genetic contribution by the inhabitants of the north-west British Isles presumably during the tenth and eleventh centuries when Iceland was being occupied.

However small, isolated populations such as characterized much of human prehistory depart from the theoretical model just outlined above. Whereas in large populations, the randomness of chance leads to stability in gene frequencies from one generation to the next, in small populations randomness cannot be attained. In fact in very small groups individuals may sometimes marry when in fact no possible alternative partner is available. Such marriages frequently occur among close kin, of necessity. A genetically determined condition which may be rare in a population at large may occur frequently in a particular group of kin and a high incidence of kin marriages perpetuates such a condition very effectively. Certain island populations provide good examples of isolates in this sense and Tristan da Cunha in the South Atlantic constitutes a prime example of this state of affairs.

Tristan da Cunha was occupied by a British garrison in the early nineteenth century, but after the death of Napoleon on neighbouring St. Helena the Tristan garrison was withdrawn. However, one of the soldiers remained—Corporal William Glass—and he was later joined by other men either as a matter of deliberate choice or else as a result of shipwreck and similar accidents. They were married to women who came to Tristan from St. Helena. These women were of mixed ancestry, possibly part European, and part Bushman-Hottentot among other things, and the men also were of diverse origins. Glass was a Scotsman; others of the men were American; others Italian and so on. In all there are now seven surnames represented in this island population which at present numbers approximately 300 individuals, so that it is perfectly evident that the degree of inbreeding is very considerable. In fact most of the islanders can trace blood connections with one another along several different lines. As a result of the evacuation of the island after the volcanic eruption there a few years ago, it was possible, in England, to undertake a complete survey of the islanders, including an examination of their state of health, nutrition, their dentition, social behaviour and anthropological features such as eye and hair colour, and genetic factors also. Many suffered from asthma, for example, and large numbers were affected by various genetical factors, including Retinitis pigmentosa, a condition found extremely infrequently in most populations but here occurring very commonly as a result of isolation and inbreeding. The Tristan population is perhaps a replica of early human populations, both in size and in the isolation factor and it is in such conditions that genetic factors become fixed in distinctive frequencies in populations, some of which were later to expand and to become the races of man. Small, inbred, and isolated groups of this kind must have constituted the original American Indian peoples, wandering into that continent across the Bering Straits from about 20,000 years ago. Once in America the isolation and inbreeding frequently continued with the result that there are still dramatic gene frequency differences between closely adjacent Indian tribes. Isolation in this sense implies breeding isolation, and this may be effected by environmental barriers such as deserts, mountains or seas. It may also be effected by social barriers including prescribed rules governing marriage, or by cultural barriers including religious and linguistic factors. Thus gypsy groups examined in various European countries manifest distinct similarities in blood groups and other features with the gypsy peoples still living in their Indian homelands and marked dissimilarity from surrounding European populations.

TABLE 4. ABO BLOOD GROUPS

Population	Number	% Blood groups			
		O	A	B	AB
Hindus of Northern India	2357	30.2	24.5	37.2	8.1
Hungarian Gypsies	925	28.5	26.5	35.3	9.6
Hungarians (non-gypsies)	1000	35.7	43.3	15.7	5.3

This is so despite the fact that for some hundreds of years they have lived among genetically quite distinct people in Europe. Social barriers have in this case maintained the genetic individuality. Again, Jewish groups which became widely dispersed in the early years of the Christian era still manifest marked differences when compared with the peoples among whom they have lived for centuries. In addition, these groups, particularly if small and inbred, became very pronouncedly distinct from one another also. Many of these long-dispersed Jewish groups have now returned to Israel where a great deal of work is being done in investigating their physical characteristics. In addition the modern state of Israel contains a long-established isolated population, a group of some 380 individuals who call themselves Samaritans. They trace their ancestry back over a period exceeding 2000 years, to the fifth century B.C. when, as a religious sect, they broke away from the mainstream of Judaism. The once numerous Samaritans now survive at Shechem (Nablus) where, during the nineteenth and early twentieth centuries, the total population comprised only some 150 individuals. Dr. Batsheva Bonnè (1965) writes: "Partly because of the aversion of Jews, Christians and Muslims toward them, which causes them to live in almost complete isolation, and partly because of their own preferred customs, the Samaritans remained strictly endogamous from a few centuries B.C. to the present day."

This population consists of five patrilineages and it is growing in number. Some 84 per cent of the matings are between either first or second cousins and the mean coefficient of inbreeding for the present generation, 0.069, is the highest yet recorded for any human community. For some of the genetic and physical traits examined, but not for all, the Samaritans have, as a result of isolation, diverged markedly from the surrounding populations. Thus they show an exceedingly high frequency of blood-group O and, very unusually, more A_2 than A_1 individuals. The percentage of non-tasters of P.T.C. is, at 6.4 per cent, very small. Among Samaritan males the enormously high value of 27.7 per cent with colour vision defects (colour blindness) was established. Bonnè writes:

Comparison of blood group frequencies as well as other genetic markers . . . indicate that the Samaritans are unlike any of the existing surrounding groups whom they might be expected to resemble. From comparison of anthropometric data the Samaritans appear to exhibit their own "typical" features which do not resemble those of any other Jewish or non-Jewish community in the Middle East. . . . Theoretical estimates of random drift in a population of such range of effective size (29.7% of the Samaritan population constitute the breeding parents, that is, the effective population) were computed and suggest that drift is likely to have had an important effect on the gene frequencies observed.

However, "Because of the relative stability reflected in gene frequencies" from one generation to the next, "it is suggested that drift is being counteracted by other evolutionary forces, such as selection pressures". Certain selection pressures were examined but no specific effect on the distribution of phenotypes and genotypes could be detected. It is suggested that in the long term, the rate of change of gene frequencies is slow and most of the selection is concerned with stabilizing rather than changing gene frequencies. It is possible that inbreeding has proceeded for such a long period that many of the inbreeding effects have been eliminated and the population has rid itself of many of its undesirable genes.

TABLE 5. DISTRIBUTION OF DIEGO POSITIVES

	Number	Percentage
Caingang, Brazil	48	45.8
Caribs, Venezuela	121	35.5
Maya, Central America	363	17.6
Japanese	65	12.3
Koreans	277	6.1
Apache, North America	73	4.1
Alaskan Eskimo	241	0.8
Lapps	433	0.0
Polynesians	80	0.0
Australian Aborigines	162	0.0
U.S.A. Whites	1000	0.0
Asiatic Indians	75	0.0
W. African Negroes	775	0.0
Bushmen	114	0.0

Other blood-group systems now known include: Rhesus, MNSs, P, Kell, Duffy, Lutheran, Sutter, Diego, Lewis and Kidd. Each of these is inherited independently of the others and each is characterized by particular antigens or blood-group substances on the red blood cells. Again the anthropological interest lies in the fact that the genes are irregularly distributed among the races of man and that many of them are known to have associated selective advantages or disadvantages to confer in given environmental circumstances. There is perhaps no necessity for giving in detail here an account of the distribution of these blood groups nor for presenting at length an account of their inheritance. However, one or two salient points may emerge. The M gene of the MNSs system occurs with high frequencies in the American continent, whilst N is very common among the aboriginal peoples of Australia (Table 3). The Diego blood group substance occurs in high frequencies only among the South American Indians (Table 5) and with lower frequencies only among Mongoloid peoples in Asia. It is not found in Australia, Africa or Europe, and is hence sometimes referred to as the Mongoloid indicator. Other genes such as "Hunter" and "Henshaw" are virtually confined to negroes.

The rhesus system is relatively complicated, as a considerable number of genes is involved. However, it is possible to simplify matters somewhat by referring only to rhesus positive (DD or Dd) and rhesus negative (dd) individuals. The system provides an appropriate ex-ample of the operation of natural selection in human populations. Rhesus negative women (dd) married to rhesus positive men (DD or Dd) frequently bear rhesus positive (Dd) children. Such positive embryos develop within "negative" mothers who are thus on occasion stimulated to produce an anti-D antibody. Should this substance cross over from the maternal to the foetal circulation the unborn infant may be severely affected as the antibody will destroy many of its red blood cells, ultimately resulting, for many cases, in death. All such deaths occur among Dd individuals so that equal numbers of the genes D and d are removed from the population. However, the subtraction is from unequal initial totals, so that if no other factors intervene, the least frequent gene, which is virtually always d, should tend to disappear. This has in fact occurred in most of the world's populations, presumably largely because of the process outlined. Thus no rhesus negative individuals occur in America, Australia, or in most of central and eastern Asia (Table 6). The d gene is most frequent in European populations and the world's peak frequency occurs among the Basques in France and Spain. This is a slight simplification of the overall picture since a few modifying factors may in fact intervene, but none the less the selective action is much as indicated above. Compensatory mechanisms preserve the Rh negative component of the population. Thus marriages which may produce Dd (Rh positive) or dd (Rh

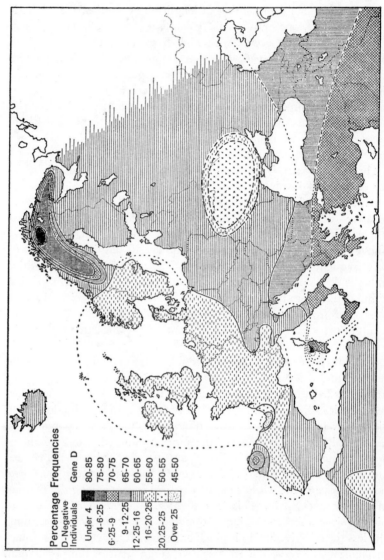

Percentage Frequencies

D-Negative Individuals	Gene D
Under 4	80-85
4-6·25	75-80
6·25-9	70-75
9-12·25	65-70
12·25-16	60-65
16-20·25	55-60
20·25-25	50-55
Over 25	45-50

Fig. 21. The distribution of rhesus negatives in Europe (after Mourant, 1954).

negative) offspring and in which haemolytic disease removes the former type, may in fact produce an excess of dd individuals. Certain rhesus blood-group combinations are highly characteristic of particular racial groups. Referring to the full rhesus terminology,* the combination c̄De (R⁰) occurs with enormously high frequency in sub-Saharan Africa, and virtually nowhere else (Table 6) whilst c̄DE and CDe combinations are very frequent in European peoples.

TABLE 6. DISTRIBUTION OF RHESUS NEGATIVES (rh or cde)
AND OF R⁰ (cDe)

Population	Number	% rh neg.	R⁰
Basques	167	28.8	0.6
English (London)	1038	15.3	2.3
Arabs (Baghdad)	300	10.3	8.3
Asiatic Indian Moslems	156	7.1	1.9
Chinese	132	1.5	0.9
Am. Indians (New Mexico)	305	0.0	0.7
Am. Indians (Mexico)	238	0.0	1.1
Indonesians	200	0.0	0.5
Australian Aborigines	234	0.0	1.3
Siamese (Bangkok)	213	0.0	0.5
S. African Bantu	300	5.3	64.3
Luo (Kenya Nilotes)	128		80.5
S.W. African Bushmen	446		78.8
S.W. African Hottentots	210		58.1

When all this blood-group material is taken together it is evident that racial groups are characterized readily enough in terms of the unique combinations of the blood-group factors which they possess. Accidental similarities in the frequencies of certain blood groups do not detract from the validity of the contention that the total constellations of genes are in fact unique in each case.

Other genetically controlled factors, in addition to the blood groups, may briefly be considered. Haemoglobin is a constituent of the blood of all individuals, the normal variety being termed haemoglobin A. However, abnormal forms also occur and these have unfortunate

* This involves three loci on one pair of chromosomes. Thus each chromosome bears one of the following gene combinations: CDE, CDe, CdE, Cde, c̄DE, c̄De, c̄dE, c̄de. Each individual has two such chromosomal combinations in his genetic constitution; for example, CDe/c̄de. Combinations involving c̄De are very prevalent in sub-Saharan African populations.

consequences for many individuals who inherit them from their parents. The best known abnormal variety is haemoglobin S. Individuals who have inherited the S gene from both parents, and who are thereby genetically SS, suffer from an incurable and fatal anaemia and they rarely live to maturity. Individuals with one normal gene, A, and the other abnormal gene, S, are genetically AS and these suffer from a mild anaemia which is non-fatal, but which reduces their

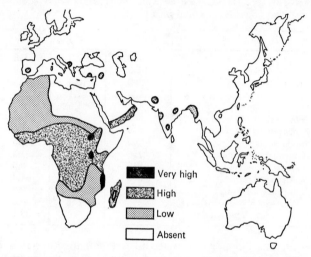

Very high

High

Low

Absent

FIG. 22. The distribution of haemoglobin S (Sickling) in the Old World.

general well-being. Given this information there would seem to be no reason but to suppose that the S gene would rapidly be eliminated from the populations in which it occurs because SS individuals do not transmit the gene since they do not live to maturity, and the AS individuals are less fit than are AA individuals. However, this elimination of the S gene does not occur, and AS individuals (having the so-called sickle cell trait; SS individuals having the sickle cell disease) occur with very high frequencies, often exceeding 20 per cent in much of sub-Saharan Africa (Table 7). It is now thought extremely likely that this is because AS individuals are far less susceptible to malaria than are the "normal" (AA) individuals and were thereby protected from one of the great killer diseases of tropical Africa certainly until the present century. A state of balance is attained and perpetuated, and this is only upset by factors such as environmental changes. Thus, if malaria is

TABLE 7. DISTRIBUTION OF SICKLERS IN AFRICA

Population	Number	Percentage
Luo (Kenya Nilotes)	294	20.4
Kikuyu (Kenya Bantu)	227	0.4
Ganda (Uganda Bantu)	3362	16.2
Pygmoid Twa (Ruanda Urundi)	141	2.8
Lunda (Angola Bantu)	600	18.2
Bushmen	500	0.0

eliminated, the advantage of the AS genotype over the AA genotype no longer pertains and one would expect that in time the frequency of the S gene would drop appreciably. This seems in fact to be occurring among the American Negroes who have for long lived in a malaria-free environment.

Other abnormal haemoglobins occur, with haemoglobin C having very high frequencies in West Africa and especially in northern Ghana; and haemoglobin E being very common in south-east Asia.

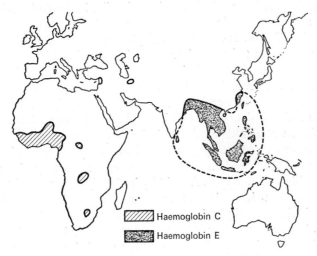

FIG. 23. The distribution of haemoglobins C and E in the Old World.

It is presumed that some selective advantage is conferred by these haemoglobins since otherwise it is difficult to account for their perpetuation. Many other blood factors, including haptoglobins and transferrins, and various enzyme deficiencies are also found differentially among human races. The inheritance of sex-linked features such as colour blindness, occurring more frequently among men than among women, is also understood. The lowest rates of colour blindness occur among hunters and food gatherers whilst the highest values occur amongst populations furthest removed from such a way of life. Intermediate values are found in populations directly dependent upon agriculture and those directly descended from hunters and gatherers. Weiner (1971) writes that "The numbers of the colour blind would tend to increase by recurrent mutations if the screening action of natural selection against them was relaxed." Pickford (1963) suggests that "The red-green blind often cannot distinguish over-ripe or rotten from ripe, or ripe from over-ripe fruit such as cherries or gooseberries from the leaves of the trees and bushes." As fewer colour-blind children or young adults died of food poisoning or gastro-enteritis, the intensity of selection against them would decrease.

The substance phenylthiocarbamide or PTC may be dissolved in water, the resulting solution being visually indistinguishable from water and also odourless. Little more than 1.3 grammes can in fact be dissolved in 1 litre and this quantity is therefore used to make up the strongest solution to be used in taste testing. Starting with the strongest solution, dilutions are made in such a way that each one is half the strength of the preceding solution. Thus the second solution contains 0.65 grammes per litre and so on. Certain, though only few, individuals find all such solutions quite tasteless and cannot differentiate the solutions from water. Others, the majority of humans, find the solutions bitter to taste, and many people find that very weak solutions containing 0.002 or even 0.001 grammes per litre are very bitter. Such remarkable variation in tasting ability is directly under genetic control, and apart from its curious and somewhat dramatic nature, it is associated with several physical conditions to which certain humans are prone. Thus among the non-tasters of PTC there is a marked excess of individuals with thyroid abnormalities and it is possible that there are similar associations between PTC tasting ability and the incidence of tuberculosis and diabetes. Again the incidence of non-tasters varies considerably among the world's populations. Virtually all the Amerindians, for example, are tasters, whilst in Europe the tasters usually constitute only some 70 per cent of the population.

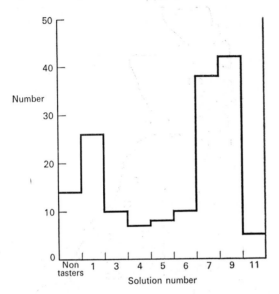

Fig. 24. PTC tasting bimodality; a sample from County Durham.

It is now perfectly evident that the races of man display marked genetic differences of all kinds and that this variability is a result of, and the means whereby, physical adaptation to the environment is achieved. However, it must be borne in mind that no race is homogeneous; in fact much variation occurs within races. Moreover, there are no sharp divides in many cases between one race and another, but rather a gradual change in gene frequencies from the one to the other. Such gradations or clines in gene frequencies are characteristic phenomena in a race context, whether on a global scale or on a much more local scale. Thus there is a cline in the gene B frequency from a maximum in central Asia to minima in Australia, America and parts of western Europe. Again, within the British Isles, similar gradations have been demonstrated.

Dr. John Beddoe (1885) showed that pronounced pigmentary variation occurred within the British Isles in hair, eye and skin colour. His work involved him in subjectively estimating the shades of colour

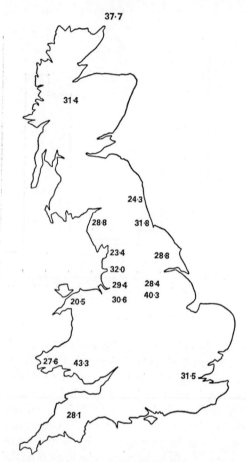

Fig. 25. England, Wales and Scotland; per cent non-tasters of phenylthio-carbamide (PTC).

which he encountered in terms of an arbitrarily selected series of scales. However, later and more sophisticated techniques, involving the use of optical instruments such as spectrophotometers, have fully corroborated Dr. Beddoe's findings with regard to hair colour, indicating that hair colour is very dark among the Welsh and very fair among the people of much of eastern England. Again, the frequency

Fig. 26. England, Wales and Scotland; per cent of the population with dark hair.

of non-tasters of PTC varies considerably from area to area in Britain (Fig. 25). Small parts of the Welsh hills, including Plunlumon and the Black Mountain of Carmarthenshire, in addition to having populations which are outwardly physically distinctive and having equally distinctive blood-group patterns, have high percentages of non-tasters of PTC, in fact exceeding 40. Over much of the country, the percentage is approximately 30, although in Northumberland and in parts of north Lancashire, the percentage is of the order of 23, whilst in parts of Derbyshire, there are more than 40 per cent non-tasters. Variation of this kind also occurs in the incidence of colour-blind males, the percentage increasing considerably from 4.92 per cent in eastern Scotland to 8.32 per cent in south-west England (Exeter). Again, recent studies have shown that skin colour is darker in South Wales than in northern England and the Isle of Man.

Physical variability of this kind is all the more remarkable in a small country such as the United Kingdom if one considers the magnitude of recent population movements which presumably have masked long-established population variability patterns. Different invasions during prehistoric and historic times did not equally affect the populations of all parts of the country and must have therefore caused the basic patterns still discernible today to emerge. Presumably the regional variation is now less pronounced than formerly but with adequate sample numbers it is none the less demonstrable. Certain rural areas have for long witnessed depopulation and have received few immigrants, so that the residual population there might still represent locally ancient genetic material. There is a qualification required, however, in that emigration is adopted by certain elements in the population and not by others, the causation being exceedingly complex. It seems likely that there is a high familial incidence in migration so that the genetic effects might similarly be familial and not random. It is difficult fully to comprehend the precise effects of this phenomenon on gene frequency distributions.

The physical differentiation of human races is not due to chance, except in the instances of small populations experiencing random genetic drift (the Sewall Wright effect); that is, chance genetic fluctuations in the breeding history of small isolated groups. More usually at present population differentiation is the result of biological adaptation by large groups of men to particular sets of physical stimuli contained in the environment. The Human Adaptability Section of the International Biological Programme (I.B.P.) aims at the

World-wide comparative study of human adaptability. The I.B.P. as a whole is concerned essentially with the functional relationship of living things to their environments . . . it is conceived as a world-wide ecological study of communities of plants and animals: those still existing in relatively natural habitats and those in more disturbed or artificial conditions. An analogous approach can be made to the ecology of mankind (Weiner, 1965).

However, biological adaptability of humans is not as directly brought about as it is in other organisms since cultural factors obtrude in such a way as to stand between man and the full rigours of direct environmental pressures. Thus, extremes of cold are not countered simply by accumulating stores of body fat and by distinctive modifications of the morphology and relative proportions of the body and the like, even though these are important factors. Cultural adaptations are also important. All the people living in Arctic North America are short, varying from 154 to 164 cm in stature means and with very few absolutely tall individuals. There is a similar concentration of short people in the northern areas of Eurasia. All the short peoples living around the Arctic seas are, moreover, uniformly thick-set. Coon, Garn and Birdsell (1950) write:

Their bodies are chunky, their chests thick and wide, their legs short and thick, their fingers and toes short, and their wrists and ankles small and fat covered. . . . Arctic peoples present the least possible skin surface area to the outside world, in proportion to volume and weight, and even that surface they keep covered, except for their faces, when outdoors in the cold. They are built to radiate as little heat as possible.

Thus there is obvious physical adaptation involved here but in addition there is a very necessary cultural adaptation also, particularly in the manufacturing of warm clothing and the creation of good, adequate homes. Only after developing adequate cultural elements of this kind could man live in the colder areas of the world, migrating there from the tropical and near tropical areas where all the early forms of man had lived, yet, as we have seen, there is adaptive physical response as well.

In the extreme, rigorous environment of the hot deserts people like the Saharan Tuareg are 'tall, lean, skinny men, with long arms and legs, short, shallow bodies and narrow hands and feet' (Coon *et al.*, 1950). Among the Tuareg, the Somali and the Australian Aborigines, for example, 'The skin surface area is great in proportion to their volume and weight. . . . The critical factor seems to be for the organism to present the maximum skin surface area in proportion to mass and weight to the external environment, thus permitting a maximum of cooling surface for evaporation." Here again, however, there are necessary, parallel cultural modifications, occasionally in clothing, as also in housing and in the organization of daily routine activity.

Perhaps the most direct interaction of man and the environmental factors most concerned are to be witnessed in simpler societies of the world. These are now found in areas of environmental extremes, and the cultural equipment and techniques, though adequate for ensuring survival, are not so sophisticated as to allow any measure of ease or any degree of effective escape from the exigencies of a close and intimate association with the natural world. The simplest human societies—the hunters, the fishermen and the gatherers of foodstuffs—can but take from the bounty provided by nature. There are very few systematic attempts made, at least in practical terms, to increase that bounty, or even in many cases to store it, so that the relationship which exists between man and the natural world about him is very close and intimate and existence basically continues on a day-to-day basis. Supernaturalism on occasion looms large in this field and societies frequently attempt to control nature to their advantage by invoking and beseeching and generally manipulating the supernatural powers whom they consider directly to control and affect the natural world. All this, however, is accompanied by a positive acceptance of the world in which man finds himself and in which he must exist and survive not only by manipulating the supernatural but also by using a series of techniques and procedures empirically known to be effective.

Grahame Clark (1961) has written that

> Environmental change was a potent agent of biological mutation, just as it stimulated migration and emphasized isolation. On the cultural side anthropological studies suggest that at any given moment of time an apparent equilibrium exists between any human society and the habitat (soil and climate) and biome (vegetation and animal life) of the ecosystem (total natural setting) in which it subsists and of which in a sense it forms an integral part: any change in habitat or biome must of necessity call for readjustments in human society of a kind involving cultural change, migration, or both, the outcome of which is the establishment of a new and likewise temporary equilibrium. It is in this continuous process of challenge and response—to use Toynbee's vivid phrase—enriched and complicated by interaction between rival societies and increasingly by contending classes—that we may surely see some explanation for the mechanics of human progress. . . .

CHAPTER 3

Social Organization

THE term "primitive" is used of certain peoples largely because their material culture—the objects which they make and utilize—is simple in form and meagre in content. Yet there is not necessarily simplicity in facets of their non-material culture such as aspects of their social life and organization, and least of all perhaps in their kinship systems. However, important and all-pervading as this may be, a detailed consideration of the latter need not be our concern here. Suffice it to say that so many facets of social life which in advanced societies are organized on a non-kinship, even impersonal, basis are in the realms of economic activity, political organization and social control generally the prerogatives of kinship based groupings in the primitive world. There is a certain intrinsic interest in examining the way of life of contemporary primitives, and their mode of existence might, at least in some respects, be regarded as illustrative of stages of development previously passed through by now more advanced societies.

Mankind has always had effectively to resolve the fundamental economic problem of securing an adequate food supply, and as was outlined in Chapter 1, the earliest solution to this basic problem was marked by dependence upon uncultivated plants, game animals, and other small foodstuffs which might be gathered. Nowhere does such a primary response now persist in unadulterated form, but its at least partial survivals in remote parts of the world, coupled with descriptions of this way of life in the early days of contact with Europeans and others, enables a summary of the major facets of such patterns of life to be established.

Some of the major groups of recent hunters and collectors were the now extinct Tasmanians, the aboriginal Australians, various pygmoid peoples in south-east Asia, including the Semang and Sakai in the Malay peninsula, certain Arctic peoples in north-east Siberia, the Congo pygmies, the Bushmen of southern Africa and many, though a minority, of the native people of the Americas. Of necessity, these people all possessed good first-hand knowledge of local food supplies, plant and animal. They possessed very appropriate tools for obtaining these foodstuffs, including digging sticks, cutting tools, fishing-hooks, bows and arrows (but not in Australia), spears and the like, though few groups possessed the whole range of implements listed. None of the artefacts was constructed of metals since these were by and large unknown to the hunting and gathering peoples. They lived in shelters, usually crudely constructed except in very cold areas; they had knowledge of fire and they cooked most of the foodstuffs consumed. Moreover, they possessed in each case a very evident social organization which, if rudimentary, crude and undifferentiated by western standards, proved sufficient for their purposes presumably for millennia. This social organization, even if rudimentary, is far more complex and sophisticated than that of the social creatures such as apes, since the social interactions possible within groups of humans are infinitely more varied than in any other creatures and are facilitated and in many instances made possible by that unique human attribute, the use of language. By this means, individual experience may become the experience of the whole group in many instances, so that there develops a body of lore, of transmitted experience and of abstract conceptualization. This remarkable cultural accomplishment occurs even among the simplest of contemporary non-literate primitive groups.

Among such groups the density of population is low, since the people do no more than extract their necessities from the (usually difficult) terrain. Everywhere in Australia internal economic specialization was limited and the Aranda, a Central Australian tribe, was no exception. All Aranda men were hunters and all women were collectors. Every individual had totemic affiliations, believing in a special bond of sentiment between the person and the totemic species whose spirit was within him. Each tribe had a fairly elaborate kinship system and all members of a tribe believed that they were related to one another. There were very few religious specialists, no groups of craftsmen, no administrative hierarchy and no legal experts who were not in each case simultaneously many other things also. Any one man could and did act effectively in a wide variety of social roles, particularly if he was a middle aged or older individual. An informant in such a society could give a social investigator a fairly full, detailed and accurate account of practically all the group's doings, concerns, hopes, views and the like. The Australian adaptation was by our standards exotic; having accepted that, its workings were clear cut and comparatively simple. Both the Australians and the Europeans have sufficiently efficient social institutions to enable them to cope with internal social stresses and disputations and to regulate their relationships with other groups.

The Aranda numbered no more than a few hundred individuals, occupying a clearly defined territory. They wandered in small groups within this territory. At each stopping place, usually in the vicinity of water holes in this arid country, wind breaks were erected for shelter. Women daily departed from the encampment and, armed with digging sticks, they searched for vegetable foodstuffs and for small animals, insects and the like, all of which were placed in a wooden, trough-like container for transporting back to the camp. The foodstuffs skilfully gathered in this way by women constituted a very important part of Aranda diet. In fact, among all the central Australian tribes collecting and gathering were far more important economic activities than was hunting. Among coastal groups (such as the Murngin) hunting and fishing were much more important for the total food supply than was the gathering of foodstuffs.

Aranda men hunted using spears, spear throwers and boomerangs. Game drives were sometimes organized and water supplies used by game were sometimes poisoned by the use of certain leaves so that the animals, and particularly emus, were stupefied after drinking and might all the more easily be caught and killed with spears. Meat supplies obtained by the men could on occasion be extremely plentiful and then be totally lacking over protracted periods. Women's contribution to the food supplies, though less spectacular, was usually far more consistently procurable. Vegetable matter might be eaten raw or else roasted in ashes. No pottery was available for any form of food processing. Meat was usually roasted in ashes.

In this basically very simple manner an adequate if meagre supply of food was procured by this people and by many others like it. This amounts to a sexual division of labour and no other, forming a simple though fairly efficient, and limited, economic basis for social activity. Everyone but the very old, the very young and the infirm participate in the all-important task of obtaining food and there are no particular specialists, although it may be recognized that some individuals are more expert than others at certain pursuits. No cultivation was practised and there were no domesticated animals other than the dog.

One is insistently conscious of the environment as one pictures the women wandering over their desolate homeland looking for roots, tubers, seeds and other foodstuffs, the men hunting the larger creatures and the camps being periodically moved from one water source to another. They were people attached to the country whose resources they fully comprehended by ties of sentiment created by "ownership" of, and familiarity with, its resources, and by their kinship with the other individuals who also lived, hunted and foraged over it. Totemism represents another aspect of their attitude towards its natural features, species and forces. These people were totally dependent on the summer rains, not always plentiful and on occasion virtually non-existent, to fill the river beds and pools and to replenish the fish and the vegetation as well as to provide quantities of fat game animals. Their relationship with and their dependence upon the environment was constant, immediate and absolute. Thus, those who share in the utilization of a region's resources must stand in an intimate relationship with one another. Common participation in the territorial rights forges powerful emotional and social bonds among individuals. Again, this special relationship between an individual and the country creates a ritual bond between a person and those natural forces and species which also occur in it. This dependence on the environment is projected back to the mythical past, in the belief that the ancestors were beings who united in themselves the qualities of man and animal or plant. Therefore totems are here a particular expression of kinship with the environment.

Aranda tribesmen each have a special relationship with a certain animal or plant species or with a natural phenomenon like wind or rain. Since they deny the reality of physical paternity, conception is thought to be effected by the spirits of animals and plants entering into women, and the children thus conceived have a precise and special relationship with the species involved, a lasting relationship ascertained by a variety of methods. Thus individuals linked to a particular species such as the kangaroo, together constitute the kangaroo totemic group in the tribe. This group, through its special supernatural relationship with the particular animal, is thought to be capable of affecting the proliferation of that animal. This is done by conducting increase ceremonies. More particularly in times of scarcity, as during prolonged drought, men of the appropriate totemic group perform these ceremonies for the specific purpose of making the animal or plant in question plentiful, so that the whole community may again have a more adequate food supply.

> The insecurity of their parasitic mode of life causes them to devote much of their time and energy to ritual activities, in which chanting, acting and dancing are combined with representational and decorative art, activities which serve to enhance group solidarity and confidence and enlist the help of unseen but creative forces (Clark and Piggott, 1970).

Some readers may feel that the simplicity of such a "primitive" response and adaptation is more apparent than real. Yet there is a simplicity in this kind of pattern which should not be obscured by the exotic nature of the society. It is a simplicity occasioned by the small scale of such societies, so that every activity within any one of them may be comprehended by any one of the constituent individuals. It is also a simplicity occasioned by the limited range of economic and social specializations. In small tribes, as in Australia and elsewhere, all the people and their doings are known to everyone else, all are kinsfolk, the daily routine is common to all, there is no internal specialization of function other than by the sexes, and the totality of environmental circumstances is comprehended by everyone. Internal disputations and external relations are dealt with by the old men, who rely upon their past experiences and their proximity to the spirit world to help them resolve the matters in hand. Hereditary rulers do not exist; effective social control and government are ultimately vested simply in the old men.

Demonstrably the hunting and gathering primitive groups lived a life which everywhere possessed certain characteristics, though there were variations in detail from one group to another. Some of these differences cannot be simply explained in geographical terms. Thus whilst the Eskimo manufactures splendid clothing, the Yahgans and some other Indians in Tierra del Fuego, again a region with a raw, cold climate, scarcely wore any clothing at all and knew nothing of the means of making it. In more general terms, explanations of material and certainly of non-material culture cannot be provided by geography alone. The culture and the social life of a group depend upon their present location to some extent but also upon their former habitats in other locations. Again contacts with other groups are sometimes very important in modifying socio-cultural elements, particularly as some peoples are very much prepared to learn from others. Much depends upon the historical experiences of the group, experiences which have moulded their basic attitudes and practices and also their "world view".

In addition to the small, simply organized, nomadic groups of hunters and collectors of food, there are larger units of cultivators and of pastoralists among whom the fabric of social life is far more intricately woven. In one sense "no human community", as Childe (1951) and others have pointed out, "is any 'lower' or 'more ancient' than any other. All represent specialized human adaptations the product of millennia of traditionalized cultural life." In another sense, however, the cultivation-pastoralist adaptation could not occur any earlier than the time of the first such adaptation in the Neolithic period.

From the original area principally in the Middle East the Neolithic cultural phase spread, but, as we have seen, even today its basic features of domestication, crop cultivation and a sedentary life in villages and urban aggregates, have not affected all the world's peoples. However, very large numbers of men are simple farmers, cultivating the soil and finding grazing for their animals in seemingly immemorial fashion. This is so among most of the tribal groups in Africa, Oceania, Central Asia and elsewhere, as it is in peasant societies also.

It is significant that in most of these more "advanced" tribal groups, and in peasant society, as among the hunters and gatherers, kinship based groupings are of great importance as means of regulating and of ordering social behaviour. The precise definition of the significant kinship groupings varies from people to people. The most significant group may simply consist of patrilineal relatives, that is of people related in the male line, as for example among the Bedouin and the Zulu. Occasionally it may be a group composed of matrilineal kin, that is of individuals related to one another in the female line, as among the Trobriand Islanders of Melanesia and the Bemba of Zambia. Frequently but a fraction of each of those groups of individuals whom we would call the father's or the mother's blood relations are of social significance. Variations in the definition of the socially significant groupings are legion but their importance, however they may be defined, is very considerable.

Among the more important kin groupings are lineages and clans. Both terms appear especially frequently in anthropological literature. For our present purposes it may be taken that a lineage is a kinship grouping which, in either the male or the female line, traces its descent from an ancestor who lived a known and usually inconsiderable number of generations back in the past. Similarly, a clan is a unilineal kinship grouping which maintains the fiction of its common descent from an ancestor who lived in the remote past and who is frequently a legendary or mythological figure. Both lineages and clans are highly significant groupings in many "primitive" societies, other than the simple hunters and collectors where such extensive kin groupings are, on the whole, rare. Jomo Kenyatta (1961) gives a precise account of the Kikuyu legend regarding the origin of their kinship system and of the clans in particular.

In the beginning the man Gikuyu, the founder of the tribe, was called by Mogai, the Lord of Nature, and given his share of the earth. Mogai also created Mount Kenya as a resting place and as a sign of his wonders, and to its summit he took Gikuyu and showed him his allotted land which at its centre contained many fig trees. This place was pointed out as a suitable site for Gikuyu's homestead. Before their parting, Mogai told Gikuyu that in case of need he could be contacted by sacrifice and by raising his hands towards Mount Kenya. On proceeding to his homestead, Gikuyu found there a beautiful wife and he named her Moombi (creator or moulder). They lived together happily and nine daughters and no sons were born to them.

Having, sadly, no sons, Gikuyu sought Mogai's advice and was told to sacrifice and then to proceed home with his family. This was done and nine handsome young men willing to marry Gikuyu's nine daughters were found at the sacred tree near the homestead. Gikuyu was hospitable to the young men and consented to their marrying his daughters but only if the men agreed to live in his homestead under a matriarchal system. This was agreed, the marriages took place and each daughter soon established her separate family. The families were jointly referred to as Moombi's family group in honour of their mother.

On the death of Gikuyu and Moombi the daughters shared equally in the inheritance of their property. As the nine groups increased in size they found it impossible to live together in one major group and so each daughter called together her numerous descendants to form one clan under her name. Thus the nine principal *meherega* clans were founded. This legendary tale is perhaps typical of many which occur in the tribal world and it serves to reiterate the realistically tenuous kinship bonds which unite the now possibly very numerous descendants of their founders.

In societies where lineages and clans as well as other kinship groupings are important, the primary allegiance of individuals may well be to that grouping into which they were born. Individuals might consider themselves primarily as lineage and clan members and secondarily as tribal men and women. Thus the emphasis upon kinship in the so-called primitive societies may in many instances militate against the appearance of extra kinship obligations and allegiances, which are necessary before states, for example, may appear. In Africa, the Lacustrine Bantu of the Lake Victoria region (Fig. 27), including the Ganda, Soga, Nyoro and other peoples, were politically highly organized. This was especially true of the Ganda. Their kings, the Kabakas, had become increasingly powerful, particularly during the nineteenth century, having done so at the expense of the kinship groupings in Buganda. In the nineteenth century successive Kabakas deliberately and successfully pursued a policy of curtailing the power of the clans and lineages, simultaneously assuming additional power themselves. As the power of such a central government waxes, so does that of kinship groupings or collectivities wane, and this process is perhaps inevitable before the fully fledged state can come into being.

Within any one state such as the Congo, many tribal groupings still exist and in such tribal groups, to an extent, the old allegiance to kin as opposed to strangers or to larger political units yet pertains—among hunters and gatherers, cultivators and pastoralists. Yet it would seem that the days of such groupings are numbered for gradually here, as elsewhere, an agricultural population is coming into being, together

FIG. 27. East Africa; the Lacustrine Bantu.

with an urban-industrial proletariat, particularly in Katanga, in which extra-kinship groupings and organizations are now of paramount importance. This situation reduplicates similar events and situations experienced in the past in Europe and North America, as well as contemporaneously in many other parts of the world.

Outside the areas of tropical forest in sub-Saharan Africa, that is, on the savannah lands, numerous tribes of cattle breeders exist, who also practise some cultivation. Examples include the Fulani (Fulbe) in West Africa, the Neur, Dinka and Shilluk in the Sudan, the Masai in Kenya and Tanzania and the Zulu and Tswana tribes in areas far to the south. In much of the area around Lake Victoria in particular, it has been argued that a substratum of hoe-cultivating groups had superimposed upon it a cattle-keeping complex introduced from areas to the north by physically distinctive and probably also linguistically different people. This scheme of things is often labelled "The Hamitic Hypothesis ".

Between Lake Victoria on the east and the Ruwenzori Mountains, Lake Albert and Lake Tanganyika on the west, lies a corridor of grassland connecting the savannah areas of the upper Nile valley with the plateaux of Ruanda and Tanzania. At an indeterminate but distant time in the past, this region was entirely occupied by Bantu-speaking agricultural "negroes", with the greatest density of population in the west. Later, this corridor was the route utilized by waves of Hamitic or Hamiticized cattle-keeping people in their southward migrations. They are reputed to have derived from southern Ethiopia and may have been of Galla origin, and they are said to have been crowded out of their homeland.

Wherever these pastoralists settled in regions already occupied by the Bantu agriculturalists they made a uniform adaptation—they conquered the agriculturalists and established themselves as a ruling class over them. Thus in the corridor one found pastoral rulers and agricultural serfs, the former often termed Bahima or Bahuma; the latter Bairu or Bahera. This type of situation pertained, for example, in the native states of Bunyoro, Toro, Ankole and Ruanda. Attractive as this scheme may seem as a means of explaining some of the salient features of social life in this area, in view of recent archaeological, anthropological and linguistic research this "hypothesis" is in fact less and less credible as an explanation of prehistoric occurrences.

These livestock-keeping agricultural tribes share many cultural attributes. A wide variety of crops is grown, the most important being certain varieties of sorghum and millet. Cattle are of great economic and social significance. Milk, and occasionally blood, are favourite foods, though beef is rarely eaten other than when animals die or are ceremonially slaughtered. Many of these tribes, however, have an extraordinary interest in and passion for cattle. The possession of large numbers of cattle confers prestige on their owner and the quality of the creatures is of comparatively little significance.

Certain of the cattle-breeding tribes are almost totally nomadic, as are many of the Fulani and the Turkana. Others, particularly in eastern and southern Africa, frequently have fairly permanent villages. The nature of the settlement pattern will depend upon a variety of factors. Professor Lucy Mair (1962) writes: "The ways in which people are distributed on the ground must obviously affect the way in which their government is organized, particularly when they (Nuer, Dinka, Shilluk and Anuak) have no means of long-distance communication." Moreover, in the four examples cited the pattern of settlement is in each case different, showing how with a simple technology, slight variations in the geographical environment are very important. This situation constitutes a variant conclusion to that which was earlier written of the interrelationship of culture and environment.

Before giving a brief account of a representative Middle Eastern pastoral tribe, let us, however, briefly continue with Africa. Traditionally, Black Africa was the home of hoe cultivators, particularly in the tropical forest zones, with the notable exception of the non-agricultural pygmies in the Congo, and of the pastoralists already mentioned, who, however, often combined hoe cultivation with their predominantly pastoral interests and pursuits. Plough cultivation does not seem to have extended further southwards than the Mediterranean coastlands, Egypt and highland Ethiopia.

Tribal groups practising hoe cultivation in the forest zones were very numerous. Examples include the Yoruba and Ibo in Nigeria and most of the Congo tribes, together with the Mende and related tribes in Sierra Leone. Large nucleated villages occurred in many of these tribes. A variety of crops was grown, including bananas, yams, taro, millet, manioc and maize. Domesticated animals were few and usually of indifferent quality and only dogs and chickens were common. Domestic herbivores were few, partly because of the incidence of the tsetse fly and partly because of the poor quality and limited areas of pasture. Hunting, gathering and fishing have been used to supplement the crops grown. Even so these tribesmen have, by and large, a protein-deficient diet. In the main, therefore, the traditional practice has been shifting agriculture. It is basically a facet of the general Middle Eastern Neolithic practices which has penetrated to these regions; and the overall complex has been largely modified, principally by environmental difficulties affecting livestock.

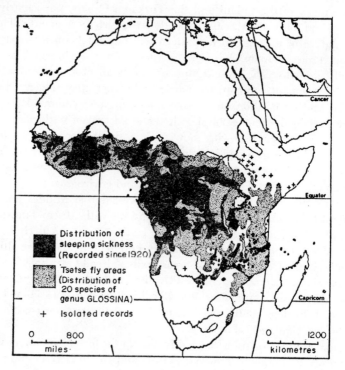

Fig. 28. Africa; the distribution of sleeping sickness and tsetse fly (after Stamp, 1965).

Thus sleeping sickness, or trypanosomiasis, for example, is a major factor, associated as it is with the tsetse fly of the genus *Glossinia*, which in turn is effectively restricted to certain habitats. *Glossinia palpalis*, the most significant species, can exist only in forests or at least in the shadow of riverine tree zones in otherwise grassland areas. Its survival is also dependent upon high levels of atmospheric humidity, and therefore dense trees with accompanying lianas and epiphytes constitute an ideal habitat. The fly is attracted to animals and to humans and in biting them prior to blood sucking it introduces into their circulation an elongated, motile protozoa, *Trypanosoma gambiense*. This multiplies and lodges in the brain causing lethargy, paralysis and often death. Severe outbreaks with high mortality rates have occurred in parts of tropical Africa. Ford (1970) cites the Soga people of southern Uganda as an example, since they were involved in the terrible sleeping-sickness epidemic in Uganda between 1901 and 1908 in which some 200,000 individuals died out of a total population at risk of some 300,000. In 1890 southern Busoga was densely populated and covered with banana gardens. The first cases of sleeping sickness were diagnosed in 1901 and it was estimated that 20,000 Soga died by 1902 and 100,000 by 1905. In 1906 the surviving population was evacuated and the banana gardens gave way to forest-savannah mosaic which became populated with elephant, buffalo and various other animals including bushbuck and bushpig and their attendant parasites. Sleeping-sickness evacuations between 1906 and 1914 caused the tsetse-fly belts to increase in Uganda, and this interrupted the recovery of cattle numbers from the very low totals reached after the disastrous rinderpest epidemics of the 1890–1900 period, when some 95 per cent of the cattle had died. Later, in Busoga "the collision between the expanding cattle population and the bush fly resulted in a reduction from 158,000 head in 1935 to 88,500 in 1949". The period 1935 to 1939 saw in Busoga as elsewhere a maximal contact of tsetse fly and cattle and the downward movement of cattle numbers was not effectively halted until a mass drug treatment was implemented from 1950 onwards. "Conditions for an epidemic in the human population and for an epizootic in the domestic livestock were maturing during the thirties and when contacts were established both appeared." In areas of tropical grasslands and on plateaux areas below 1200 metres, two other species of trypanosomes are associated with varieties of the tsetse fly which flourish in less humid air, though still in the shade of trees and bushes.

Quite evidently population density is usually low in regions of fly-infested forest, and in primitive conditions extensive forest clearance for fly-control purposes could not be accomplished, even if its efficacy were realized. Both domestic cattle and many wild creatures often succumb to the disease and so in large parts of tropical Africa few cattle may be reared with consequent effects upon the economy and the use of resources generally. However, the ecology of trypanosomiasis is complex.

In the great proliferation of books about Africa it is not uncommon to see references to the supposed effects of tsetse fly. More than one eminent prehistorian has invoked Glossinia as a controlling mechanism for Stone Age migrations. The evidence is flimsy. In West Africa breeds of cattle have developed which are tolerant of infection and dense human populations have grown up in spite of endemic sleeping sickness. In East Africa cattle populations have more than doubled during a period in which the tsetse fly belts have expanded by many thousands of square miles. Almost all modern human ecology in tropical Africa has to be studied in the light of the catastrophic epidemics and epizootics which followed upon the European invasion, and this applies equally to the social effects of trypanosomiasis (Ford, 1970).

Pastoral nomadism, with very little cultivation, is widespread in steppe and desert areas. In such regions grazing and water supplies are sufficient to maintain the animals only if they are periodically moved to new areas. Traditionally, nomadism of this kind was found in arid regions extending over much of north Africa through many Middle Eastern areas and so to Central Asia. Representative peoples included the Saharan Tuareg, various Bedouin tribes of the Arabian peninsula and the Kirghiz of Central Asia. This way of life may have been a relatively late offshoot from the plough-farming culture of south-west Asia and might well have commended itself as a more efficient method for utilizing the resources of uncultivable areas.

Thus the Rwala, the most powerful of the 'Anaza group of tribes, occupy steppe and semi-desert areas in the Arabian peninsula and occasionally, after periods of rain, briefly utilize the grazing in the desert areas, which they may also traverse during their migrations. This tribe has some 3500 tents and it migrates in the eastern part of the 'Anaza territory, from areas south and east of Damascus where the summer is spent, to the periphery of the Nefud and the northernmost oases of central Arabia. The annual migration route is approximately circular. Having endured "the weary and long agony of summer" near Damascus from September onwards, they migrate south eastwards over the hamad (tracts of coarse grasslands) and in spring they move southwards to the fringes of the Nefud sandy desert and to the vicinity of Teyma oasis. In early summer they move north and west along the Sirhan depression and reach their tributary villages before the maximal heat and drought of summer. The precise migration route and the speed of movement will vary according to the distribution and the frequency and amount of rainfall.

The welfare of the camel herds is the prime determinant of the migration schedule. Normally small groups of Rwala migrate from pasture to pasture with their animals and only very rarely do large numbers of tribesmen join together. The camel is splendidly adapted to living in these harsh arid conditions, since it can store reserves of fat and moisture in its hump and needs to be watered infrequently particularly if the vegetation is green. Forde writes: (1957) "The camel is the fundamental source of wealth, for not only does it supply food and valuable materials, but it is the only important marketable thing that the Badawin have." It is the means for obtaining all manner of goods which are not produced by the tribesfolk themselves, including weapons, clothing and supplementary food supplies.

A Badawin camp is usually pitched fairly near a water supply which is central for a range of pastures. Herdsmen take the animals daily to the nearest pastures but once these are exhausted the herds must be taken to more distant pastures where they and the attendant herdsmen may remain for periods of days and even weeks.

Camels' milk is the major food, and for prolonged periods the only food supply. A she-camel may give between two and ten pints of milk daily, according to the quality of the pasturage. It is consumed either fresh or sour and it may be stored. Not only is the camel an indispensable beast of burden in the desert, but the hair is a very important raw material for ropes and weaving, tent cloth and waterproof cloaks and the hide is used for bags and bottles.

Despite its far lesser economic significance the horse is nevertheless very much prized. It is ill-suited to living in deserts and requires constant care in order to ensure its survival. Yet no one who aspires to any social standing is without one.

Important foodstuffs obtained from sedentary communities include wheat, barley, rice, dates, salt and coffee, and wild products such as fruits, tubers and bulbs are also collected as food. Locusts are gathered when they appear and they constitute a storable supply of food. Meat is rarely consumed, camels being killed only on special occasions.

Game animals are caught, but their meat constitutes but a minor part of the total food supply.

It is clear that animals are of the utmost importance for their human owners, who are highly skilled at finding pastures and water for them. The necessary nomadism occasions an absence of permanent settlement although through the centuries these nomads have had all manner of social contacts, both peaceful and otherwise, with sedentary dwellers in the villages and towns within reach along the migration routes. In many areas where this way of life is found, existence is precarious. The vagaries of rainfall are such that frequent droughts may occur and in cases of severe drought, nomadic tribesmen may lose their herds and subsequently be unable to continue their traditional way of life. In this event, sedentarization may well occur.

Transhumance, as practised in parts of Europe and the Middle East, for example, constitutes a variant of pastoral nomadism proper. It implies seasonal movement of livestock by settled people. In parts of Switzerland and Norway, the uphill summer movement is short and the herds are near home. In other parts of Switzerland, many people move long distances up and down with the herds, the permanent village being located on low ground. In areas of the Balkans the permanent village may be in the high summer pastures. In medieval Wales cattle were moved up to the hill pastures in summer, the summer residence being the "hafod", whilst the permanent habitation, "hendre", was on lower ground. Movements of this kind imply migration by a minority of the community only. Economically it maximizes the efficiency of resource utilization and provides a high protein diet for the community for much of the year.

The nomadic tribesfolk of the Old World deserts have periodically erupted explosively into the world of the sedentary farmers. For a variety of reasons including climatic fluctuations on the one hand and political dissension and over-population on the other, the arid pastoral habitat has on occasion failed adequately to provide for its human occupants. These have then, fired by great religious fervour, possibly developed because of the harshness of their uncompromisingly hostile territories, moved out into the world of the sedentary communities. There they have conquered and plundered and there too they have in time acquired many of the sophisticated habits and attitudes of the sedentary populace and have abandoned the life of the wandering pastoralist completely. The seventh century and subsequent expansion of the Arabs, originating with Mohammed, is perhaps the classic instance of this pattern of events. Other examples include the eleventh-century Turkish and the thirteenth-century Mongol expansions in Asia. For protracted periods, great new empires founded in this way, hammered at the doors of Europe, sometimes to be successful but often eventually, and after many vicissitudes, repulsed. Frequently portrayed in European literature as barbarian, they provided a measure of political stability within their confines which allowed a highly civilized way of life to develop and within which trade and the arts, among other things, flourished.

It is interesting to consider how all this remarkable diversity of human organization came into being. One cannot accept race as a determinant of human behavioural and organizational patterns. In 1799 Charles White, an English surgeon, wrote of the white, European race (also termed Aryan, Teuton and Nordic) and of its superiority in particular: "Where else shall we find that noble arched head, containing such a quantity of brain? . . . Where that variety of features, and fulness of expression; those long flowing, graceful ringlets; that majestic beard, those rosy cheeks and coral lips?" Again Günther (1927) wrote: "Degeneration (that is, a heavy increase in inferior hereditary tendencies) and denordization (that is, disappearance of the Nordic blood) have brought the Asiatic and south European peoples of Indo-European speech to their decay and fall; . . . threaten the decay and fall of the peoples of Germanic speech" . . . "Judgement, truthfulness and energy are qualities always found in Nordic man." National policies implying the existence of racially inferior elements in various states are still pursued, and Hitlerite Germany perhaps provided the outstanding recent example of racism run riot. In *Mein Kampf*, Hitler presented his version of racialism. The human race, he maintained, contains three categories: founders, maintainers, and destroyers of culture. The Aryan or Nordic race, to which the Germans were held to belong, consisted of founders and maintainers, whilst the Jews only contained destroyers. The Germans were to unite racially for a struggle to the death with the Jews, since, Hitler claimed, history showed that whenever Nordic blood was mixed with that of inferior peoples, the result was the destruction of the culture-sustaining race. No credence can scientifically be accorded such extravagant statements.

In the past Ratzel and Huntingdon have, among others, argued that human social differences are due to, or at least are closely linked to, environmental factors. Their view emphasized "the sovereign influence of environment". Yet crude environmentalism also fails satisfactorily to explain these human differences and it is evident that non-geographical factors must also be considered. As Firth wrote (1958): "Man is helped in attaining relative freedom from his environment by his high degree of mobility, his inventiveness, and his power, especially through the facility of language, of borrowing ideas and applying them to change his condition."

A starting-point is perhaps provided by assuming that the nature and organization of a human group is basically the result of a series of adaptations by the people involved, over many generations, to the natural environment in which they find themselves. This is true at least to the extent that certain broad limitations and curtailments of activity are afforded by virtually all environments. Professor K. Little (1951) has indicated in writing of the Mende people of Sierra Leone that there is a positive acceptance of the world as it is, coupled, however, with the view that it is for man to attempt to mould that world to the best possible advantage to himself. Thus within this generality of environmental limitation there are many discrepancies and exceptions. The first and obvious need is to explain why certain possibly extensive areas with a similar environment are utilized very differently by the human populations living there. How is it, for example, that cattle keepers and cultivators may share precisely similar environments in East Africa? Of course, instances may well be quoted to indicate the still powerful grip of environmental pressures. Areas of the world are even today uninhabited because of the harsh conditions, climatic or otherwise, found there. Other areas are very difficult to utilize. The Eskimo and the central Australian Aborigines still remain within the firm hold of environmental dictates. However, the limitations in environmentalism have long been recognized by a majority of geographers and other social scientists. Again particular imperatives are imposed by some environments such as an essential extensive nomadism in the arid areas utilized by North African pastoralists. Evidently, many socio-cultural activities must stem from direct environmental imperatives, and certain geographical effects on social life undoubtedly remain; but one cannot, as Firth has pointed out, even in simple societies crudely invoke and interpret the sovereign power of the environment. Man is rather an active factor in selecting responses and in changing and modifying the environment, which in its altered form may still influence man in return.

Human socio-cultural variability may again partly be understood in terms of other factors such as the migrations of peoples, taking with them their ideas, implements, customs and institutions either to similar or quite different habitats, contacting other human groups in the process. Diffusionist ideas experienced their hey-day towards the end of the nineteenth century and the beginning of this century. Diffusionists believed that cultural change and progress were mainly due to borrowing, in situations of culture contact. Particularly in recent centuries, though not always so, the contacts have been of an advanced, complex, large-scale, Western-style society with small-scale, pre-literate, technologically simple societies. Thus Lebon (1952) writes: "Fuegians, Bushmen and Australian Aborigines have remained as exemplars of the first human economy because of geographical isolation, bred of the great distances which have separated these peoples, until recent times, from the knowledge of more elaborate techniques and social organization which have been evolving elsewhere." He points out that in addition to distance, physical obstacles also may add to the problems of intercommunication.

In contact situations it may be that whilst certain ideas and institutions are borrowed, others are rejected. Again some tribal groups may borrow and adapt readily whilst others, even if nearby, borrow not at all and remain unchanged despite the "contact". Thus in *African Cultures* (Bascom and Herskovitz, 1962) Ottenburg has written of the Nigerian Ibo receptivity to change.

> The Ibo are probably more receptive to culture change, and more willing to accept Western ways, of any large group in Nigeria. The receptivity to change is explicable in terms of many factors. Thus, the high population density has affected physical mobility and adjustment to new conditions. Ibo culture is a changing culture and is particularly adapted to some aspects of European culture. This people has had a measure of contact with Europeans for some three centuries and even before then it was unlikely to have been a totally static society.

Despite the individual ghastliness of slavery, early contacts with Europeans were friendly. Once the slave trade was abolished, it was replaced by trading in palm products. The British conquest caused little internal disorganization, and did not initially destroy Ibo culture or its indigenous system of leadership. In fact this leadership decayed because the British did not utilize it in the framework of colonial administration, thus leaving the way open for new types of leaders to emerge.

In the same work Schneider has written of Pokot (Suk) resistance to change. This is a Nilo-Hamitic tribe in western Kenya. Schneider

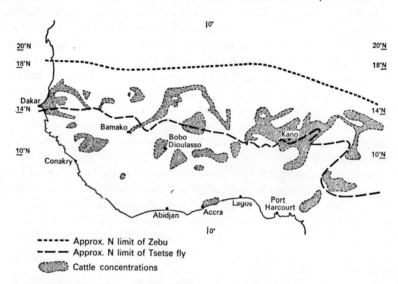

Fig. 29. West Africa; the distribution of cattle concentrations (after Harrison Church, 1957).

believes that lack of receptivity to change has causes based upon the cattle complex and an essentially pastoral way of life. The cattle complex is in fact the focus of Suk society—"it is the central, all encompassing value". Despite devastating cattle plagues such as rinderpest, cattle are less affected by drought and disease than are crops in this area, since cattle are mobile while crops are not. Even more important for the Suk, as for other Nilotic and Nilo-Hamitic people, is the fact that cattle, sheep and goats increase without too much care being devoted to them. Pastoral life therefore provides security through the accumulation of numbers of animals. Again among the Suk "all the diverse elements seem to be mutually compatible and to function with a minimum of friction. A change in any element might produce a chain reaction of adaptation within the culture and the Pokot have succeeded thus far in resisting innovations which would have this result."

Warfare was a very important activity among the pastoral Niolotes and Nilo-Hamites of East Africa. Herd losses could thus be recouped, wealth increased and young men could achieve renown and fortune. These people were the terror of the more sedentary groups. Thus these pastoralists felt an intense pride in their way of life, a certain superiority over neighbouring, different, groups and a fierce desire to maintain a life that made this possible.

It would appear that, in some instances anyway, the complex of ideas, customs, institutions and value systems are so inextricably inter-woven in one social fabric that they become as a complex immutable or certainly very difficult to change. This may be so in new social or environmental circumstances, and the very nature of the "primitive" socio-cultural situation may militate against movement into new parts of the world or change in the present locale. It may be that social inertia accompanies geographical inertia. It is surely inconceivable that a predominantly pastoral people on the East African plateau should migrate into the Congo Basin, not simply because of environ-mental factors but also, to put it in other terms, because a whole way of life would have to be so modified as to become virtually meaningless for the people. If the customary large herds of cattle cannot be kept, then the associated ritual, attitudes and systems of values also disappear, the social fabric is torn and a meaningful existence becomes impossible.

Yet migrations have occurred, perhaps in many cases because of exceptional or uncontrollable circumstances. The causation may lie in natural calamities, crop failure, animal diseases, warfare, internal dissension, expanding population, among other factors. Among the southern Bantu peoples of Africa, such as the Tswana, tribal migrations were common and the population was, to a large extent, mobile. There is evidence which indicates that this mobility, both here as well as in other parts of Africa, is of long standing and, as a result of such movements, peoples must have acquired much knowledge of matters previously unknown to them. In this way social factors and cultural attributes may become widely disseminated. It has been argued that similar artefacts and similar ideas, beliefs and customs indicate that the people who possess these similarities were once closely associated in some way and have subsequently moved apart. This interpretation is in accord with most diffusionist ideas. Others have argued that such similarities are frequently due to chance inventions and innovations in two or more human groups being to all intents and purposes identical. It is probable that there is some validity in both contentions, together with the certainty that even in the "primitive" world peoples did have some systematized contacts with one another, in some instances over considerable distances.

However, anthropologists and others who have studied human groups in the pre-literate world frequently tend to give the impression in their writings that the people among whom they lived and with whom they may be intensely conversant, constitute an isolate, a primitive isolate, with the most meagre of contacts with other peoples. This may in some instances be an unintended impression but it none the less exists. It would often appear that a tribal group described in a monograph seems to exist quite unmindful of neighbouring tribes and other groups in the world about them. Redfield, especially, shows that by emphasizing singularity the primitive isolate is valuable as a conceptual model, as a means of organizing ideas and facts about a people, free from the complexities of having to consider other peoples in direct association with them. Apart from this it would seem that the value of the isolate concept is minimal since it is increasingly evident that people everywhere, to some extent, have had contact with others, either systematically or sporadically, and the isolate is thus very rare. Some such contacts may be very few as were those of the Polar Eskimo in northern Greenland, but their situation was highly exceptional. In the Melanesian islands lying north-east of eastern New Guinea the *Kula* institution involved the ritualized exchange of *soulava* (necklaces) and *mwali* (shell bracelets or arm-bands) among individuals on many islands over a considerable area. Associated with this activity much trading and economic exchange occurred involving pottery, sago, stone adzes and other items. Moreover, the human contacts effected could transcend island and tribal confines.

Allowing that human contacts have existed for very many centuries and that the contacts have allowed the flow of ideas and information to take place, the transmission by such means may nevertheless be slow and inefficient. As has been outlined, between some 9000 and 10,000 years ago men living in well-ordered groups in the Middle East domesticated animals, cultivated crops, learnt the expertise of pottery and later mastered the techniques of metallurgy. It is known from archaeological evidence that these revolutionary practices, which

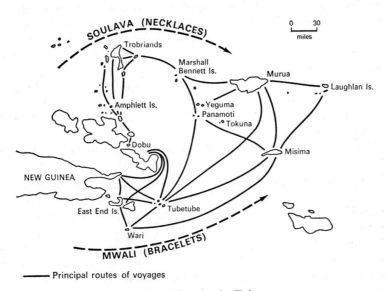

——— Principal routes of voyages

Fig. 30. Melanesia; the Kula.

appeared in a world otherwise totally utilized by hunters and collectors of food, spread from that area in most directions. Yet none of these remarkable achievements was found in Australia before Europeans arrived there; the people of the Pacific Islands had no knowledge of metal working, and hunters and gatherers still survive in the Kalahari region of south-west Africa. It required the technological advances of modern industrial Europe to make possible the rapid spread of a standard, European, white civilization to so much of the world, a spread unprecedented either in extent or in its rapidity. No part of the world remains now utterly unaffected by European peoples and their ways. Military personnel, missionaries, technical experts, voluntary workers, administrators and traders live among the Eskimo in Arctic North America and in remote parts of Africa. The Soviet Union has actively encouraged its European population to spread into parts of Siberia not long since solely occupied by aboriginal tribes. For centuries, the peasant way of life in the Russian steppes competed with pastoral nomadism, since on these grasslands, both ways of life were efficient means of utilizing natural resources. Thus permanent expansion of cultivation into these areas could not occur until after the pastoralists were controlled by military force. The Russian expansion eastwards was a long-drawn-out matter occupying many centuries. Wolf (1966) writes: "The expansion was spurred by fur traders and ore prospectors rather than by cultivators proper, and it has only been in this century, under Communist leadership, that an effort has been made to conquer Siberia for agriculture, this time under conditions of post-peasant technology."

Economic changes now occur in all parts of "Darkest Africa", largely instigated and maintained by European capital and technical direction. Moreover, Australian extensive farming utilizes the Aborigines' hunting grounds. It would seem that the white man's ways if not the man himself are now ubiquitous. Yet this expansion of the European world, mainly trans-Oceanic, is really a phenomenon of only the last few hundred years. Two series of events, sometimes termed the Agricultural and the Industrial Revolutions, are intrinsically part of a sequence of which Europe's expansion is itself but a part. We have already noted the enormous significance of the first, Neolithic, agricultural revolution. The second agricultural revolution, largely originating in Europe, paralleled the Industrial Revolution's development, especially in the eighteenth century. Thus Wolf writes: "It was the Industrial Revolution, with its new sources of energy and its new bodies of knowledge, which gave the new agriculture its essential impetus."

This, second, agricultural revolution witnessed the year-round cultivation of arable land, involving the development of crop rotation and the use of fertilizers. Improvement of drainage and the weeding of crops also became very important. Plant and animal breeding were applied widely and systematically. New crops from other parts of the world were introduced and specialization of production concentrated in certain areas. New machinery was introduced into farming on an ever-increasing scale.

With so much innovation the immutability of traditional methods of land-holding and land utilization was questioned. Agriculture was rationalized and became an economic enterprise aiming at maximal output rather than, as before, constituting a way of life with associated subsistence and ceremonial attachments. The world of that great mass of humanity, the peasants, was rapidly and, in some instances, drastically changed, even obliterated.

CHAPTER 4

Peasants

"Peasantry . . . is that style of life which prevailed outside of the cities and yet within their influence during the long period between the urban revolution and the industrial revolution" (Redfield, 1959). Such a style of life implies some harmony of parts and some continuity through time, the generations looking over their lives both in the past and in the future.

The second agricultural revolution diminished the significance and importance of the peasantry since it did not any longer produce the major part of the rents and profits on which the emerging social order had been at first based. A certain specialization of production had of course occurred among the peasants themselves. Goods not consumed by the peasants might be produced and then exchanged for foodstuffs and goods imported from elsewhere. But as the economic processes evolve the comparative self-sufficiency of the peasant way of life disappears and a new specialist appears, in a world becoming increasingly specialist.

Peasant society is sometimes described as "midway between the primitive tribe and industrial society" (Wolf, 1966). Peasants are neither primitive nor modern but "They are important historically, because industrial society is built upon the ruins of peasant society. They are important contemporaneously, because they inhabit that 'underdeveloped' part of the world whose continued presence constitutes both a threat and a responsibility for those countries who have thrown off the shackles of backwardness" (Wolf, *op. cit.*).

Marketing, of course, provides an efficient means of effecting peasant interchanges, particularly for exchanging specialist items of production for others not locally produced. Thus many eastern Chinese peasants produced rice and also they kept silkworms for the manufacture of silk thread for marketing. It would seem that there, as in so much of the world, life could not be adequately supported solely by agricultural production for direct consumption.

Wolf has described three types of domain traditionally affecting the peasantry: patrimonial (feudal), prebendal (bureaucratic), and mercantile. With patrimonial or feudal domain over land, control of the occupants of the land is placed in the hands of lords who, as members of kinship groups, inherit that control. This control implies the right to receive tribute from the inhabitants in return for their occupancy. However such a system is organized in detail, the peasantry always provides the basal level of society.

There is no inheritance factor in prebendal domain. In this case domain is granted to officials who draw tribute from the peasantry in their capacity as state servants. They therefore receive grants of income (prebends) in return for the exercise of a particular office. Remuneration of this kind was important in strongly centralized bureaucratic states such as Sassanid Persia, the Ottoman Empire and traditional China.

A third major form of domain is mercantile domain, with land viewed as the private property of landowners. This property may be sold and purchased and used profitably by the owners. An over-right to land is asserted with an implied right to collect tribute (rent) in return for its use.

The three forms of domain over land are not usually mutually exclusive; they usually coexist. The components which do coexist, and their relative proportions, determine the "organizational profile of a particular social order" (Wolf, *op. cit.*).

Many general attributes of peasants everywhere may be clarified by particularly referring to the Middle East. Throughout this region the population may be divided into three discrete and fundamental occupational entities: pastoral nomads, sedentary agriculturalists and urban specialists. Within each of these, members share economic, social, political and ideological similarities which cut across linguistic, political and religious differentiations. The "social distance" as well as differences in detail of culture content obtaining between herder, peasant and urbanite in the Middle East is frequently extreme and each is in a very real sense only a partial participant in the totality of the culture in which he finds himself.

The Middle East peasant group has a number of distinct attributes. It is economically based on the specialized production of cereal crops, with secondary or regional concentration upon the production of vegetables, fruits and cash crops such as cotton or tobacco. There is a low level of technological development with normative dependence on man, animal and water power. Therefore there is a high ratio of man hours of labour per unit of production. This in turn restricts internal economic diversification and the increase of total content and diversity within peasant culture as a whole. Where an appreciable surplus is possible even with a simple technology it is commonly found that this is drained off from the village level by urbanite absentee landlords. The capital sums required for economic development are not available within the peasant communities themselves.

The social organization of the peasants usually involves residence in compacted villages where the major patterns of interpersonal relations are defined in cross-cutting terms of co-residence and kinship. Such villages are defined by a high degree of particularism or *campanilismo* but it has not been clearly demonstrated that the tendency for intra-village marriage has been essentially related to the difficulties of communications and that this is breaking down with involvement in wider networks of relationships due to better roads and to automative transport.

Characteristically in many parts of the Middle East the fundamental socio-economic unit is the extended family, calculated patrilineally, and the maximal kinship unit is the lineage. Thus Stirling writes (1965):

> ... Kinship relations are the single most important set of relationships outside the domestic group, and a very high proportion of activity is kinship activity. ... Different kinship roles do not carry specific and distinct rights and duties, but rather a general duty of affection, help and support. The general lack of specificity and the optional and variable character of kinship ties make the kinship system amorphous, without making it unimportant.

Writing of lineages, he states that

> Their existence and persistence does not rely on the part they play as units in a larger system, but on the recognition and fulfilling of the special personal rights and duties of agnates to each other. It is the fact that the men of a number of households recognise both close relations of a general kind and the specific duty

to defend each other that constitutes the group. This group is much more obvious in a crisis when faced with an active quarrel and the possibility of violence.

Participation in the beliefs and practices of a formal religion, usually a sect of Islam, is highly valued, but knowledge of the actual content of the particular faith is limited and unsophisticated and extra-orthodox accretions cause considerable regional variation. Thus, for example, the Druze who are numerous principally in Lebanon, Syria and Jordan, are basically Shi'a Muslims whose beliefs also incorporate the deification of the Fatimid ruler Hakim, coupled with mystical and concealed non-Islamic beliefs.

In a more general sense Robert Redfield, who carried out much of his own field work in Mexico, was much concerned with the interrelationships of peasant (folk) society and urban society, and basically conceived of this interrelationship in terms of a continuum where folk and urban society constituted the two poles. Redfield's scheme defines an ideal type, the folk society, which is the polar opposite of urban society. The ideal type is a mental construct to which no actual known society precisely corresponds. It exists only as a model since its formulation may suggest aspects of real societies which deserve and require study. This folk type of society was defined by Redfield as small, isolated, non-literate and homogeneous, with a strong sense of group solidarity. Ways of living are conventionalized into that coherent system which we call "a culture". Behaviour is traditional, spontaneous, uncritical and personal; there is no legislation or habit or experiment and reflection for intellectual ends. Kinship, its relationships and institutions are the type categories of experience and the familial group is the unit of action. The sacred prevails over the secular; the economy is one of status rather than of markets. Using his Yucatan material, Redfield implied the hypothesis that loss of isolation and increasing heterogeneity are causes of disorganization, secularization and individualization. Should this be demonstrated to be so in reality, it would not, however, necessarily follow that these are the only causes of such effects. His view was that as the folk-type community loses its isolation, through contact with the city, it becomes more heterogeneous, a market economy develops and indications of disorganization appear.

Again, as J. Pitt-Rivers (1963) has pointed out, the study of the relation of the local community to the larger social units which enclose it has come to the forefront of anthropological thinking in recent years. Thus the peasant society has been defined as a "part-society", but part of exactly what and how related to that of which it is a part remains largely obscure; whilst, according to Pitt-Rivers, the temporal dimension of this relationship remains obscurer still. The folk-urban continuum therefore poses the considerable problem of the structural relationship between the local community and the region, city, nation and state—in fact, the outside world. Unlike the tribal society whose autonomous structure could be treated without reference to its neighbours, the peasant community's relation to outside forces can be seen to be significant in determining its internal structure. The degree to which the local community is integrated into the national structure and the mode of its integration are highly variable. Yet, everywhere, the solidarity of the community, of the kinship groups and of the extended family as social, economic and juridical entities has suffered during recent centuries at the hands of national integration. State-controlled functions have increased, as for example in responsibility for maintaining law and order; communications and economic organization have greatly extended both conceptually and territorially. Most significantly, the concept of individual ownership has grown at the expense of collective property. "The passage from relatively autonomous communities to units within an integrated state involves the destruction of pristine collectivities in favour of individual rights"‘ because the individual is one with whom the modern state can deal. His responsibilities and duties towards the state may be defined by the national law: he can simultaneously belong to both the local and the national community. However, the state cannot deal with the village collectivity nor the patrilineal descent group with equal facility.

Integration into the national economy involves adopting its standards and conventions: currency, contractual freedom, wage labour and, ultimately, investment. These are all incompatible with customary law which in turn depends upon the cohesion of collectivities. Once the viable collectivities cease to exist, individual ownership makes possible an increase in economic inequalities. This makes possible a system of patronage based upon economic power, and through this the local community may be controlled in a way quite new and unlike the control based upon hereditary allegiances or traditional leadership based on customary law. Individual ownership, to the exclusion of all other forms, appears then as a function of political and economic centralization.

When European ways are presented to the small-scale societies— tribal groups or peasant villages—either in organized form or else randomly, certain individuals appear to be far more responsive to these external stimuli than the majority prove to be. Lerner (1958) writes of the village of Balgat south of Ankara: "The personal meaning of modernisation in underdeveloped lands can be traced, in miniature, through the lives of two Balgati—The Grocer and The Chief." The Chief was content with the traditional way of life, its attendant obligations, rights, attitudes and duties. The Chief is "a vibrant soundbox through which echo the traditional Turkish virtues". However, "the Grocer is a very different style of man. Though born and bred in Balgat, he lives in a different world, populated more actively with imaginings and fantasies—hungering for whatever is different and unfamiliar. Where the Chief is contented, the Grocer is restless" . . . The Grocer said: "I have told you I want better things. I would like to have a bigger grocery shop in the city, have a nice house there, dress with civilian clothes."

As in Balgat, so in countless other small communities in many parts of the world there are men who will fairly readily accept newly professed ideas, who will modify them and adapt them to local circumstances. Other men in similar communities, in uncertain times when changes are presented to them, resist such innovations and continue instead to champion traditional sets of values, to live according to "old-fashioned" precepts. As the changes proceed, despite resistance, so the traditional standards become increasingly anachronistic. The age-old patterns of behaviour and standards of values are partially if not totally meaningless when divorced from the totality of the social systems in which they once operated and were meaningful.

A variety of circumstances may result in marked resistance to change, among them ignorance of alternative, novel forms, fear of implementing change, or else vested interest in preserving the old social order. It is frequently customary to label landowners, the rich, and religious leaders, among others, as reactionary. Such allegations were frequently made, for instance, in post-war Iran. In Iran agricultural land was owned by private landlords, religious groups, the Government and the Shah, as well as by peasant cultivators. Approximately one-half of the arable land was, until recent years, owned by the landlords.

> Much of the worst managed land in Iran is in the hands of the biggest landlords. Typically they are absentees who give little thought to improvement or the welfare of the peasants, and entrust management to professional overseers who may ruthlessly exercise their power over the peasants while the landlords enjoy themselves in Tehran or Europe or America (Mohammed Reza Shah Pahlevi, 1960).

Many of the smaller landowners are more closely identified with their peasant tenants and more concerned with their welfare. About one-fifth of the cultivable land in Iran is still controlled by charitable and religious trusts and it is administered largely by the clerics, with the state exercising supervisory rights. Lay managers usually manage these estates on behalf of the clergy. The Iranian Government and the Crown own a tenth of the arable land of the country. This is cultivated by the peasants, the State playing the role of landlord, either directly or else by sub-letting the land to private contractors.

The remaining areas of arable land are owned by peasant proprietors. In some villages a fraction of the land may be owned by such proprietors; in other villages, all the land is so owned. During the last decade the proportion of land owned by peasant proprietors has increased steadily and considerably. By the mid-1960s, "Over 500,000 acres of agricultural land had been divided among some 25,000 villagers" (Pahlevi, *op. cit.*, 1960). The usual practice was for land owned by the Crown, the Government and landlords to be partitioned into small units, each big enough to support a man and his family. This land was then sold at prices below market values, to the cultivators, who paid for it over a number of years. The rate of land transference was partly determined by the rapidity with which ancillary services could be provided, including tractors, water supplies, roads, agricultural advice and the like. Quite evidently the Iranian peasantry had much to gain by this process and one can certainly vouch for the eagerness with which the peasants awaited the allocation of land in their own villages. Naturally many private landlords and clerical owners of land opposed the land reallocation policy. Many of these individuals fel that they had much to gain by maintaining the old social order whereby they received large incomes from their estates. This opposition was politically well organized, and the clerical leaders in particular were able to bring mobs on to the streets of Teheran on many occasions, in an attempt to modify by such unconstitutional means the policy of land allocation. These mobs were partly bribed to act, partly coerced and partly used by individuals and parties who hoped thereby to overthrow the ordered government of the Iranian state.

> Only a few years ago these landlords became very bitter when anybody broached the idea that their vast holdings should be divided, but many have now come to realize that in terms of social justice their position is untenable. Moreover, with the expansion of alternative investment opportunities, land owning as such no longer commands quite so much profit or prestige value as formerly. Obsolete production methods are commonly in use on the great estates, and the introduction of modern techniques would require heavy investments, so that many landlords are finding that they can get quicker returns from investing in Persia's expanding industry and commerce (Pahlevi, *op. cit.*, 1960).

Yet the land-allocation programme continued.

While one must agree with the social justice of giving land rights in this manner to the peasants, it should be borne in mind that some measure of education was essential so that the peasants should become, however remotely, familiar with wider social horizons and, it was hoped, more responsive to the need for improved agricultural practices. An adequate educational programme, as was intensively launched in the Persian countryside, coupled with land reform, can solve many of the problems, economic and social, of mid-twentieth-century Iran. It is likely that had this evolutionary process been prevented by reactionary elements in the State, landlords or clerics, a far more drastic even revolutionary sequence of events might have occurred.

Peasant society in Iran, as elsewhere, has certain characteristics which serve clearly to demarcate it. It is a society in many ways intermediate between the tribal way of life and urban society; between the primitive and advanced societies. Peasants live on the land and yet they have a close and enduring relationship with urban groups, with gentry and with townspeople. They are organized in small-scale communities which are parts of larger and complex social and cultural entities. Peasants are small producers for their own consumption. For them, agriculture is a livelihood and a total way of life and not simply a business for profit. Agriculturists who carry on their agriculture for investment and business, looking on land as capital and a commodity, are farmers and not peasants.

The peasant has control over a certain plot of land to which he is strongly and for long attached by tradition and sentiment. He need not own the land, he need have no particular form of tenure and he need not have any particular type of institutional relationship with either gentry or townsfolk. All that is required is that the so-called peasant group should have such control of the land as to allow its members to carry on a common and traditional way of life into which their agricultural activity intimately enters, but not as a business enterprise for profit. Once the agricultural activity involves a business-like attitude, we have entered the realms of commercial farming.

Such peasant groups, tilling the soil, do not exist in social isolation. They have definite, clear-cut relations with a social élite such as, in historical times in Europe, manorial lords and urban dwellers. The peasants are dependent upon this élite for social support and protection and, provided that this support is forthcoming, the whole system remains viable and even flourishing.

Some readers may be more or less familiar with a peasant-type society at first hand. There are, moreover, numerous written descriptions of the peasant way of life. Arensberg and Kimball (1940) described Southern Ireland as a country of small farms, the greater part of the farming families supporting themselves on from 15 to 30 acres, living off the land and selling their surplus product, for such necessities as flour and tea. The farmers run their farms on the labour of their families though they receive some help from their kinsmen. This situation provides an example of small-scale social situations, clearly delimited economic activity, the absence of business-like commercial farming, with the whole peasant system simultaneously geared to providing some of the needs of and to receiving certain reciprocal duties and services expected of an urban community. Commodities produced on the land may be sold in the towns and permanent social arrangements for doing this usually exist. Other social needs such as the necessity of providing spouses also serve effectively to link together the peasants and the urban classes. A basically similar situation, with some modifications, exists in rural Wales (Rees, 1950) and in this country there is much published material to demonstrate the emergence of a peasant–lord relationship out of the tribal background.

A perhaps less familiar example is provided by the peasants of Central Iran. Apart from a few regions, Iran is an arid country, with great stretches of desert and semi-desert particularly on the interior plateau (Fig. 31). In this environment, a most important factor

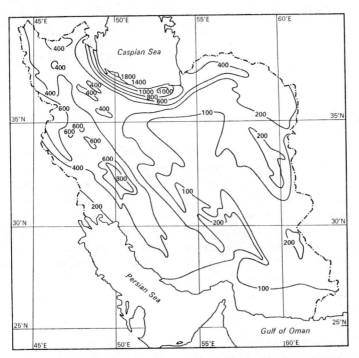

Fig. 31. Iran. Mean annual amount of precipitation (millimetres), 1951–60 (after Ganji in Fisher, W.B., 1968).

influencing the location of cultivation and thus of settlement is water availability. Where water is available, all is verdant, cultivation is the rule and flourishing communities exist. In the absence of water, there is very little vegetation and these areas are either uninhabited or else utilized by pastoralists, either village based or else tribal and nomadic. In Iran as a whole the cultivated areas are small and scattered and these isolated patches of land are tilled by men using rather primitive techniques. As a means of expanding the cultivable area water may be brought for tens of miles in *qanats*, underground tunnels which tap the water table and convey the water to lower altitudes by gravitational flow. These devices are very widespread and elaborate throughout many parts of Iran.

There are locally dense village settlements in the high valleys of the isolated mountain ranges, usually in fairly close relation to a large town in the plain below. Thus the uplands of Kuhistan, centring on the Shir Kuh south-west of Yazd, have nine large villages with a peasant population once estimated at 27,000. In summer these villages serve as the *yailaks** of the citizens of Yazd and then double or treble their population. Thus some 80 kilometres south-west of Yazd and located high up in the mountains is the village of Tezerjan. It has a population of some 2000 people (5000–6000 in summer owing to the influx of Yazdis), and unlike most Iranian villages, which are nucleated, it is a settlement strung out along the banks of a number of small streams draining outwards from the high ground. The mountain upstream from the village has some ice and snow cover through much of the year so that the streams are rarely completely dry, although the flow is minimal in summer. The water provided by these streams makes cultivation possible and a thriving community feasible.

Houses owned by the villagers are generally small and may consist of one room only, supplemented in most cases by a courtyard, the scene of much domestic activity, an outhouse which serves as store and kitchen and a flat roof which is the summer-time sleeping place. Each family has such a house, and these are constructed by local people using equally local raw materials, particularly poplar poles, brushwood stones and mud. In Tezerjan there are some more substantial houses owned by Yazdis and occupied by them more particularly in summer, when they escape from the heat of the comparatively low-lying city of Yazd (*ca.* 1250 metres) to the very much higher and therefore cooler village.

As stated, there are a number of other villages in these mountains, each one, in certain basic features, resembling Tezerjan itself. The

* *Yailak, yailaq* or *sardsir* are terms for summer quarters used by certain Iranian peoples.

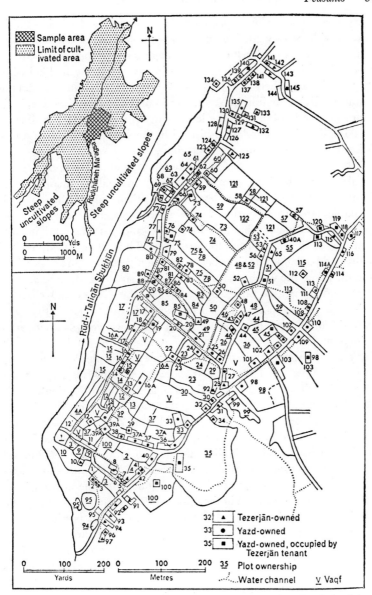

FIG. 32. Tezerjan; land-owning in an Iranian village (after Sunderland in Fisher, W.B., 1968).

villages are separated from each other by many miles of arid land which only provides scanty grazing for village- owned goats and sheep.

To some extent, therefore, each village forms a discrete social and economic entity. Some of the peasants in Tezerjan own the land which they cultivate; others are tenants who till the ground for absentee landlords, living mainly in Yazd. Yet in all cases there is a deeply felt enduring relationship with the land of the village. There is a timelessness implicit in the relationship with the land, a continuity from father to son through many generations.

Whenever the water supply is abundant, most of the village land is cultivated. This is so after heavy winter snowfalls and spring rains. Should the water supply be less plentiful, then only a fraction of the available land can be tilled. The stream water is diverted along specially constructed channels into fields and gardens, and it either continues to flow away from the stream until it is all absorbed, or else it is directed back into the river bed and then diverted again further down stream. When the water ceases to flow in the stream bed, wells are sunk there and the water raised by hand into the ditches and channels. It is a simple method of crop irrigation that is fairly effective when water is comparatively plentiful, but it involves a complex network of irrigation channels and great fragmentation of the land holdings. In dry years it is evidently difficult to allocate the available water among so many cultivators. To be denied water in one's fields is a very serious matter since it may result in destitution, and so the allocation is settled by all the adult men meeting together and discussing the situation under the direction of the village headman. When words fail, blows sometimes succeed in resolving issues, and occasional gifts of cash to the headman may assist in bringing matters to a satisfactory conclusion in so far anyway as some people are concerned. In Tezerjan, as in much of Iran, the 1950–63 period was dry and much peripheral land in the village area was unutilized in the mid-1960s. The methods of cultivation are simple. In spring the land is manured as much as possible and the ground is dug using long-handled spades—there are no ploughs. Crops grown include wheat, potatoes, some vegetables: radishes, lettuces and onions, together with a variety of fruit trees, among them mulberry, apple, pear, cherry and plum. The wheat is ground at the village mills all of which are driven by water power, and wheaten flour made into bread, which, together with the items listed, constitute the basic diet for most people. This is supplemented by small quantities of meat, eggs and milk products, particularly soured sheep and goats' milk, the delicious *mast*. Small surpluses of these commodities are sold and the cash income used to buy, in particular, tea and sugar, paraffin and some items of clothing.

The basic economic unit and indeed the fundamental social unit in Iranian peasant society is the family. Extended kinship groups may be partially recognized as such but they have little significance in matters of real concern. Spooner (1966) reports that

> In Persia, society is bound together almost exclusively by the personal relation-
> ship, which takes the form of a deep, unquestioningly loyal friendship and provides
> the links between families, which are the basic units of society. The only thing a
> man can definitely rely on outside his own family circle is such a friendship,
> which naturally becomes the more intense because of the greater need of social
> security, which in a western society is provided rather by institutions and a
> relatively sovereign respect for the law.

Despite the strong sentimental attachment to the valley, the village, and the land in general, many people either choose or else have to sever this connection. Considerable numbers annually leave the village and become taxi drivers, factory hands, manual workers in the oil fields, etc.; they become urbanized. The total population of the big cities of Iran, and particularly of Tehran, has increased dramatically since the 1939–1945 war, and the increase is for the greater part due to the denudation of the population of the country-side. Some of the peasants leave their villages for the winter months only, but in either event the causative factors seem to be economic difficulties together with social dissatis-faction. Without drastic economic reorganization, particularly by in-creasing available water supplies, it is unlikely that Tezerjan and many villages like it can support many more people than at present.

The people of Tezerjan are aware of much wider social possibilities than are found within the confines of the valley. Thus, the urban élite of Yazd who spend much of the summer here, the engineers, lawyers, dentists, doctors and business men, employ local people as house-servants, cooks, gardeners and general handymen. These two groups have close social and economic relationships which serve at least to show the villagers that other ways of living, other foods, other habits:

in fact, that other worlds of experience exist around them. Again, there are schools in Tezerjan, one for boys and another for girls. The teachers are provided by the literate classes in the towns and again, by individual precept and example as well as by the subject matter taught, new ideas are introduced. Villagers who have left Tezerjan for the cities return periodically and retell their experiences in detail to all and sundry. By such means there is knowledge of the Shah's land-reform plans, of the oil nationalization programme in Messadeq's day, of the visits of foreign rulers to Iran; in fact, of all manner of events from the bigger world outside Tezerjan and its counterparts.

Knowing of other and better social conditions there is, perhaps inevitably, some measure of discontent with current conditions in Tezerjan, crudely verbalized into comments such as "Why should the landlords have so much of the produce of these large gardens, while we own no land and receive a pittance?"

The seeds of change are germinating among the peasants. In the absence of powerful outside influences working for change, the peasant system with its comparative self-sufficiency and social limitations can endure, but once the seed of discontent is sown by an awareness of things different from and perhaps better than those of the villages, some resultant change is probably inevitable. New consumer demands among the peasants are stimulated by the precepts of the élite, and these may only be satisfied by acquiring additional cash. Perhaps the most obvious way of obtaining this is by moving elsewhere and selling one's labour, as many do; otherwise, in the valley itself by obtaining good agricultural land (as they hoped to do when the Shah turned his attention to the land problem in this part of Iran) and exploiting land, not so much as peasants but as commercial farmers. It is true that peasants cannot overnight become commercial farmers but such a transition, be it gradual or rapid, seems very likely in many parts of Iran.

Just as, in much of Iran, the rural peasantry provides numbers of people to swell the populations of the urban centres, so, in smaller parts of the country, tribes of pastoral nomads now, as for many years past, provide individuals who settle as peasants in villages. It is frequently reported that the nomads were healthier and more virile than the peasants who, in turn, were frequently decimated by epidemics and other natural calamities. The increasing nomadic population could therefore find places to settle in parts of the country periodically incompletely utilized by the sedentary populace. In this sense sedentarization was always possible.

In addition, sedentarization occurred as the result of variable economic conditions among the nomads. As in peasant society, so also among the nomads, each family constituted an economically independent unit. Should that unit find itself in economic difficulty as a result of some disaster affecting the flocks and herds, it could not remain nomadic; sedentarization was forced upon it. Without adequate numbers of sheep and goats, nomadism as a way of life is impracticable. Since alternative means of subsistences are impossible in the nomadic tribes, the impoverished nomads settle as landless peasants in villages, usually near the tribe's migration route.

Alternatively, by good fortune and good management, the livestock owned by some families might increase considerably. Large flocks and herds are precarious forms of wealth, and some of the animals were habitually converted into less risky commodities such as jewellery, carpets and, above all else, land. Land was purchased in villages along the migration route and let to tenants under a variety of agreements. Rents were usually paid in kind, that is, in agricultural produce, so that the rich nomad need not now sell animals in order to acquire agricultural foodstuffs. Consequently livestock numbers progressively increase. Once, as a result of this process, when land became the paramount form of wealth, it required to be adequately controlled and its utilization by tenants supervised, and there was a pronounced tendency for the rich nomad to establish himself as a landlord in a village; he became sedentary. Any subsequent herd disaster simply completed his divorce from the nomadic way of life with its attendant attitudes, sets of values and ideals, and the sedentarization process is completed.

It is perhaps evident that in Iran and in much of the world in general, culture change, though a process of long standing, is progressing apace. Traditional responses by human societies in different environments are in a state of flux, as a result of factors inherent in the societies themselves as well as because of outside influences which impinge upon them. As yet, the traditional responses persist in many parts of the world and they may continue for many years in those parts where the environment makes alternative responses difficult. Any alternative to extensive nomadic pastoralism as a means of utilizing the natural resources of much of the Iranian plateau is difficult to envisage. Yet, over vast areas of the world, change, and very rapid change, appears to be the keynote. Culture change is the process by which the existing order of society—its organization, beliefs and knowledge, tools and consumer goods—is more or less rapidly transformed. Changes are induced partly by factors and forces of spontaneous initiative and growth and partly by the contact of two different cultures.

We have briefly looked at the emergence of man, in Africa, from a pre-human background and at his racial diversity. We have also looked at his social development during the many millennia of his pre-agricultural phase. The revolutionary episode of the Neolithic era has been examined and the spread of the new way of life, principally from the Middle East, has been indicated. The scope and extent of this diffusion of social and cultural factors have varied spatially and certain regions were little affected by these factors, even into the twentieth century. The least affected of the world's peoples, the hunters and gatherers, are intrinsically fascinating, and moreover they provide glimpses of a way of life once ubiquitous in the world. They have been glimpsed as the curtain descends on the last throes of their existence; their prehistoric forerunners are dimly and inadequately perceived through the shadows of the numerous overlying centuries. In much of the world they have been totally superseded by pastoralists and particularly by cultivating and peasant communities in which social changes, largely emanating from Europe, are now occurring rapidly and systematically. A certain measure of uniformity of socio-cultural patterns seems inevitable in the not too distant future, as communications improve and as cultural and social innovations spread from region to region thus obscuring the differences between them; but one feels that the world, although presenting more equal opportunity for all, will none the less become, in its greater uniformity, a far less interesting world in which to live.

References

AMMERMAN, A. J. and CAVALLI-SFORZA, L. L. (1971) Measuring the rate of spread of early farming in Europe. *Man* **6,** 674–88.

ARENSBERG, C. M. and KIMBALL, S. T. (1940) *Family and Community in Ireland*, Cambridge, Mass.: Harvard University Press.

ASHLEY MONTAGU, M. F. (1951) *An Introduction to Physical Anthropology*, Thomas.

BASCOM, W. R. and HERSKOVITZ, M. J. (1962) *Continuity and Change in African Cultures*, University of Chicago Press.

BEDDOE, J. (1885) *The Races of Britain*, Bristol: Arrowsmith and London: Trübner.

BONNÈ, B. (1965) A genetic view of the Samaritan isolate, Ph.D. Thesis, Boston University Graduate School.

BOYD, W. C. (1950) *Genetics and the Races of Man*, Oxford: Blackwell.

BUETTNER-JANUSCH, J. (1966) *Origins of Man*, Wiley.

CHILDE, V. G. (1951) *Social Evolution*, London: Watts.

CLARK, G. (1961) *World Prehistory—an Outline*, Cambridge University Press.

CLARK, G. and PIGGOTT, S. (1970) *Prehistoric Societies*, Penguin Books.

COLE, S. (1959) *The Neolithic Revolution*, London: British Museum.

COON, C. S. (1961) *Caravan. The Story of the Middle East*, New York: Holt and Co.

COON, C. S., GARN, S. M. and BIRDSELL, J. B. (1950) *Races. A Study of the Problems of Race Formation in Man*, Springfield: Thomas.

DAY, M. (1965.) *Guide to Fossil Man*, Cassell.

EYSENCK, H. J. (1971) *Race, Intelligence and Education*, Temple-Smith with New Society.

FIRTH, R. (1958) *Human Types: an Introduction to Social Anthropology*, New York: Mentor.

FISHER, W. B. (ed) (1968) *The Land of Iran*, Cambridge University Press.

FORD, J. (1970) Interactions between human societies and various trypanosome–tsetse–wild fauna complexes. In: *Human Ecology in the Tropics*, ed. J. P. GARLICK and R. W. J. KEAY, Pergamon.

FORDE, C. D. (1957) *Habitat, Economy and Society*, London: Methuen.

GÜNTHER, H. F. K. (1927) *The Racial Elements of European History*, London: Methuen.

HALLOWELL, A. I. (1962) The procultural foundations of human adaptation. In: *Social Life of Early Man*, ed. S. L. WASHBURN, Methuen.

HARRISON CHURCH, R. J. (1957) *West Africa*, Longmans.

HOCKETT, C. F. (1958) *A Course in Modern Linguistics*, New York: Macmillan.

HOCKETT, C. F. (1959) Animal "Languages" and human language. In: *The Evolution of Man's Capacity for Culture*, ed. J. N. SPUHLER, Detroit: Wayne State University Press.

KENYATTA, J. (1961) *Facing Mount Kenya. The Tribal Life of the Gikuyu*, London: Mercury Books.

103

KOPEĆ, A. C. (1970) *The Distribution of the Blood Groups in the United Kingdom*. London: Oxford University Press.

KURTÉN, B. (1972) *Not from the Apes*, London: Gollancz.

LEBON, J. H. G. (1952) *An Introduction to Human Geography*, London: Hutchinson.

LERNER, D. (1958) *The Passing of Traditional Society: Modernizing the Middle East*, Glencoe, Ill.

LITTLE, K. L. (1951) *The Mende People—a People in Transition*, London. Routledge and Kegan Paul.

MAIR, L. (1962) *Primitive Government*, Penguin Books.

MOHAMMED REZA SHAH PAHLEVI (1960) *Mission for my Country*, London: Hutchinson.

MOURANT, A. E. (1954) *The Distribution of the Human Blood Groups*, Oxford: Blackwell.

NAPIER, J. (1971) *The Roots of Mankind*, London: Allen & Unwin.

OAKLEY, K. P. (1951) *A Definition of Man*, Science News, No. 20, Penguin Books.

OAKLEY, K. P. (1966) *Frameworks for Dating Fossil Man*, Weidenfeld and Nicolson.

PICKFORD, R. W. (1963) Natural selection and colour blindness. *Eug. Rev.* **55,** 97–102.

PILBEAM, D. (1970) *The Evolution of Man*, London: Thames & Hudson.

PITT-RIVERS, J. (ed) (1963) *Mediterranean Countrymen*, Paris: Mouton.

REDFIELD, R. (1959) *The Primitive World and its Transformation*, Ithaca: Great Seal Books (Cornell University Press).

REES, A. D. (1950) *Life in a Welsh Countryside*, Cardiff: University of Wales Press.

SAUER, C. O. (1969) *Agricultural Origins and Dispersals*, Cambridge, Mass. and London: The M.I.T. Press.

SCHULTZ, A. H. (1962) Some factors influencing the social life of Primates in general and of early man in particular. In: *Social Life of Early Man* (ed. S. L. WASHBURN), Methuen.

SNYDER, L. L. (1962) *The Idea of Racialism*, Princeton, New Jersey: D. van Nostrand Co. Inc.

SPOONER, B. (1966) Iranian kinship and marriage. *Iran* **4,** 51–59.

STAMP, L. D. (1965) *The Geography of Life and Death*, Fontana.

STIRLING, P. (1965) *Turkish Village*, London: Weidenfeld & Nicolson.

TIGER, L. and FOX, R. (1972) *The Imperial Animal*, Secker & Warburg.

TOBIAS, P. V. (1961) The meaning of race. In: *Race and Social Difference*, ed. P. BAXTER and B. SANSON, Penguin Books, 1972.

UCKO, P. J. and DIMBLEBY, G. W. (1969) *The Domestication and Exploitation of Plants and Animals*, London: Duckworth.

WASHBURN, S. L. (1960) Tools and human evolution. *Scientific American* **203,** 63–75.

WASHBURN, S. L. and JAY, P. C. (eds.) (1968) *Perspectives on Human Evolution*, New York: Holt, Rinehart & Winston.

WEINER, J. S. (1965) *International Biological Programme; Guide to the Human Adaptability Proposals*. Naples: Giannini.

WEINER, J. S. (1971) *Man's Natural History*, London: Weidenfeld & Nicolson.

WOLF, E. R. (1966) *Peasants*, Englewood Cliffs, New Jersey: Prentice-Hall Inc.

Index

105